WILD EDIBLE PLANTS OF THE MID-ATLANTIC

LOCATE, IDENTIFY, STORE AND PREPARE YOUR FORAGED WILD PLANTS

FORAGE AND FEAST SERIES: COMPREHENSIVE GUIDES TO FORAGING ACROSS AMERICA

BOOK 1

SHANNON WARNER

Rowan's

PUBLISHING

ALSO BY SHANNON WARNER

Individual Regions:

Wild Edible Plants of the Mid-Atlantic

Wild Edible Plants of New England

Wild Edible Plants of California

Wild Edible Plants of the Pacific Northwest

Wild Edible Plants of Texas

Wild Edible Plants of the Great Lakes *(Coming Soon)*

Wild Edible Plants of the Great Plains *(Coming Soon)*

Wild Edible Plants of the Southeast *(Coming Soon)*

Wild Edible Plants of the Gulf Coast *(Coming Soon)*

Wild Edible Plants of the Upper Midwest *(Coming Soon)*

Wild Edible Plants of the Rocky Mountains *(Coming Soon)*

2-in-1 Guides:

Wild Edibles of the West Coast (California & the Pacific Northwest)

Wild Edibles of the Northeast (Mid-Atlantic & New England)

Foraging the Wild South (Texas & the Southwest)

Foraging the Midwest *(Coming Soon)*

Foraging the Southeast *(Coming Soon)*

Foraging the North *(Coming Soon)*

CONTENTS

Foraging Overview   ix

PART ONE
WHY FORAGE?

1. The Benefits Of Foraging   3
2. Ethics and Legality   5

PART TWO
THE MID-ATLANTIC STATES WE ARE VISITING

3. Delaware   9
4. Maryland   11
5. New Jersey   13
6. New York   15
7. Pennsylvania   17
8. Virginia   19
9. West Virginia   21

PART THREE
FRUITS AND SHRUBS

10. Allegheny Blackberry   27
11. Autumn Olive   29
12. Beach Plum   31
13. Bearberry   33
14. Black Elderberry   35
15. Northern Highbush Blueberry   37
16. Chickasaw Plum   39
17. Dog Rose   41
18. Hardy Kiwi   43
19. Japanese Barberry   45
20. Nannyberry   47
21. Northern Spicebush   49
22. Pawpaw   51
23. Persimmon   53
24. Purple Passionflower   55
25. Red Chokeberry   57
26. Red Mulberry   59
27. American Red Raspberry   61
28. Woodland Strawberry   63
29. Wineberry   65

PART FOUR
HERBS AND GREENS

30. American Pokeweed   69
31. Black Cohosh   71
32. Bloodroot   73
33. Blue Violet   75
34. Burdock Root   77
35. Chickweed   79
36. Chicory   81
37. Dandelion   83
38. Garlic Mustard   85
39. Ginseng   87
40. Goldenseal   89
41. Japanese Knotweed   91
42. Jerusalem Artichoke   93
43. Mallow   95
44. Mugwort   97
45. Ostrich Fern   99
46. Pineapple Weed   101
47. Pink Wood Sorrel   103
48. Plantain (Greater)   105
49. Purple Deadnettle   107
50. Purslane   109
51. Sassafras   111
52. Staghorn Sumac   113
53. Watercress   115
54. Wild Garlic   117
55. Wild Ramp   119
56. Yellow Sweetclover   121

PART FIVE
TREES AND NUTS

57. American Beech   127
58. American Hazelnut   129
59. Bitternut Hickory   131
60. Black Cherry   133
61. Eastern Black Walnut   135
62. Butternut   137
63. Chinese Chestnut   139
64. Shagbark Hickory   141
65. White Oak   143

PART SIX
MUSHROOM AND FUNGI

66. Safest Way to Cook Mushrooms   147
67. Entoloma   149

68. Black Chanterelle   151
69. Blewit   153
70. Chanterelles   155
71. Chicken of the Woods   157
72. Giant Puffball   159
73. Hen of the Woods   161
74. Honey   163
75. King Bolete   165
76. Lobster   167
77. Oyster   169
78. Shaggy Mane   171
79. White Button   173
80. White Morel   175
81. Witches' Butter   177

PART VII
Poisonous Plants   179

PART VIII
Preparing for Feast or Famine   183

PART NINE
BONUS RECIPES

82. Nannyberry - Maple Butter   189
83. Beach Plum Jelly   190
84. Berry Jam   191
85. Raspberry Syrup   192
86. Elderberry Liqueur   193
87. Infused Dandelion Vinegar   194
88. Purple Dead Nettle Tea   195
89. Frozen Blackberry Yogurt   196
90. Shagbark Hickory Syrup   197
91. Shaggy Mane Ink   199
92. Pawpaw Bread   200
93. Strawberry and Japanese Knotweed Crisp   201
94. Pickled Hen of the Woods   202
95. Pickled Rosehips   203
96. Stir-Fried Greens   204
97. Porcini Risotto   205
98. Butternut Pesto Pasta   206
99. Jerusalem Artichoke Soup   207
100. Chicken Ginseng Soup   208
101. Creamy Fiddlehead Soup with Chives   209
102. Old-Fashioned Black Walnut Cookies   210
103. Burdock Root Decoction for dogs   211
104. Black Trumpet Soufflé   212

Conclusion   213

PART TEN
APPENDIX
The Universal Edibility Test   217
Glossary   219

About the Author   223
Bibliography   227

FORAGING OVERVIEW

One crucial question you should ask is, "**why bother?**"

The answer is, "why not?" Most of you will say grocery stores and malls are a pain, but they're convenient. You can get what you need when you need it, but this isn't always true, is it? Foraging for yourself is a feeling that one can't put into words; it allows you to claim unique ownership of what you cook and eat. Spending time outdoors alone or with your family isn't just lovely; it's also satisfying knowing that you can feed them healthy, safe food you picked yourself. Have you ever found that the conveniences of modern life are sometimes as much a curse as a blessing?

Picture these two scenarios and decide which one fits you best:

1) You're walking through a mall or grocery store on a weekday morning, listening to the buzz of the too-bright fluorescent lights and bumping into people who are also looking at their shopping lists.

2) You are outside. The sun is shining, the birds are singing, and you're foraging for the best that nature offers. The work might get dirty, but you're doing something valuable and productive. You know that whatever you find will be seasonal and healthy, like nothing you can get in the stores.

Maybe those scenarios are a bit of an exaggeration, but hopefully, you get the idea. Modern life has given us so much, but it's also chipped away at us. The good news is that there are other, more straightforward, simple ways to live your life that don't rely so heavily on malls and superstores.

Simple doesn't mean unfulfilling. Arguably, the opposite is true. While humanity has, in some respects, sought to become a separate entity from nature, there's an inherent flaw with this way of thinking.

Humans' DNA is hard-coded to interact with nature. We are hunter-gatherers. We explore the natural world, whether roaming through forests or climbing trees to find the next delightful bounty out there. This desire to wander and forage what we need has never gone away. It wasn't long ago that humans survived off the land, and there's no real reason why that should change. You could argue that it's even more critical for people to reclaim their past.

No, this doesn't mean you should forsake modern life entirely and live in the wilderness. Fearing the unknown is hard, but foraging is not. Foraging allows you to live a different life and take advantage of what nature offers by living off the land sustainably.

Nature isn't that far away. You don't need to travel miles to a distant state or another country. All you have to do is walk out your back door. This book focuses on the Mid-Atlantic region of the United States, so, as you'd expect, it'll help you find some of the best edible food you can forage in this area. Once you know what you're looking for, go for a walk or a hike and find a feast of fantastic food waiting for you to take home and turn it into something truly extraordinary. You can make some unique and undeniably delicious dishes; all it takes is a little imagination and a willingness to get out there.

Hopefully, it's already clear that foraging your food is an entirely different experience. Dreaming about all the new things you will eat and the places you can explore in search of that food. Let's look at just a few benefits of harvesting your food.

PART ONE
WHY FORAGE?

1 THE BENEFITS OF FORAGING

First of all, it's free. Whether your grocery bill is starting to sting more than usual or not, everyone wants to save money. Foraging allows you to supplement your groceries with food that is healthy and free of all the additives you usually find in grocery stores. Foraged wild edibles are non-GMO, pesticide-free, and all-natural. They're also packed with nutrients and vitamins, not to mention unique flavors you can't find in processed farm-raised foods.

A significant issue with a lot of grocery store produce is that, often, it's either force-grown out of season or shipped from miles away. There are several problems with this. That food had to travel from another state or even another country, so its carbon footprint is enormous. Another major problem is that it just doesn't taste fresh. Let's talk about how wild foraged foods taste. Have you ever compared tomatoes bought out of season with those grown in your (or a friend's) greenhouse? The difference in flavor is almost laughable. You can only harvest wild plants at their peak, so as long as you know what you are looking for, it's always in season!

Foraged wild edibles are delicious because they're in season, but they're also delicious because they're something new and different. You often can't find these plants in the store, but they grow everywhere. Some of them taste similar to foods that you recognize. Many have unique flavors that turn a dish into something extraordinary.

Imagine cooking a dish for your friends and family and blowing them away with an exciting flavor that is nothing like they've ever tasted before. Even better, you then get to say that you harvested it yourself. It doesn't get any more homemade than that.

Finally, learning to forage safely is a worthy goal. Foraging your food allows you to be more independent and self-sufficient. No one ever plans to get lost in the wild or be thrown into a survival situation, but you never know what's going to happen while you are out on that hike, that bike ride, or walking through that field. These skills aren't just valuable; they're potentially life-saving. There is no exaggeration here; Identify edible food in the wild, even in an unfamiliar area, and Prepare it correctly, has saved lives. You're ready for the worst-case scenario and, in the meantime, enjoy some delicious and healthy free food.

The main thing that puts people off from foraging is that they don't have the skills and knowledge to do so safely or effectively. There are many delicious things to eat in nature but plenty of things you would be wise to avoid. Luckily, we're here to help. With this guide, you can be fully equipped and prepared to get out there and forage in the Mid-Atlantic region with confidence. So, without any further ado, let's get started.

2 ETHICS AND LEGALITY

F oraging is rewarding, you can find some exotic and tasty things, but there are some basics you need to learn before heading out. Let's face facts, you can eat a tasty-looking mushroom if you don't know what it is, but you may only be able to do that once.

Your top priority is understanding the health and safety concerns of foraging and the "how-to" in Identify edible plants to avoid anything poisonous. In a survival situation, it's better to go without food than to eat something that makes you sick.

Let's take a second to talk about where these glorious plants come from; without Mother Nature, there is no foraging. The importance of responsible and sustainable foraging is something everyone needs to take into consideration before haphazardly going out and pulling up plants. It means you should know how to forage ethically and consider nature conservation.

Foragers have a responsibility to not only keep themselves safe but to look after the environment. If people don't look after the natural world, it's not just the plants and animals that will suffer. Humanity will suffer as well. It's not just a moral and ethical duty to take care of the land we forage from, but we have practical reasons for doing so. With this in mind, how can you forage ethically?

Some of the following tips and principles are obvious, while others are less so.

- Only harvest what you need.
- Never pick all of a plant. Take up to ⅓ of the leaves of a plant; any more than that risks the plant's health. Please don't take a plant in short supply; let it grow before Harvest.
- Rotate your foraging areas. Not doing so may stress a habitat too much.
- Leave an area looking at least as good as you found it, take any trash with you, and don't trample plants or other natural spaces. If you brought it in, you need to take it back out.

- Replant dislodged roots and plant seeds in similar areas. Avoid introducing invasive species to a site free of them.
- Use appropriate tools to avoid doing too much damage.
- Cut leaves and stems with a sharp object instead of pulling them and risking uprooting the plant, for example. It's also easier for a plant to heal from a clean cut than a tear or twist.

Ethical foraging primarily comes down to common sense. You've probably done a good job if you haven't left too much evidence of your presence. If you focus on Harvest invasive species over rarer ones, you might even be helping out nature. As well as respecting nature while Harvest wild edibles, responsible foragers must also respect the law.

Believe it or not, you can't simply wander wherever you like and take whatever plants interest you. Foraging is a surprisingly controversial activity, depending on where you are. Each state in the United States has different foraging laws and regulations and can even differ from National Park to National Park. Foraging may not be permitted in specific locations. Other areas allow you to harvest exact amounts of a wild harvest. Some places may let you take nuts and berries but not take mushrooms or any roots.

The best way to find out the rules where you plan to forage is to ask. Check with local wildlife authorities and park authorities for information. Signposts are also your friends, but you can often find this information online before you visit an area. You don't want to discover that you're breaking the law by encountering an angry park ranger.

Another potential legal pitfall when foraging is whether the land you're Harvest from is publicly or privately owned. Here's a funny story; see if you can spot my mistake. I once enjoyed a hike in the Appalachians, the views were stunning, and it was a beautiful day. I assumed that it was a public area, but guess what? It wasn't. I ended up being chased away from the site by an angry gentleman and his equally angry dogs. It wasn't the most pleasant end to my hike, but I learned an important lesson. If there are barbed wire fences or other signs of an animal pasture, then it's probably a privately owned area. Private owners rarely appreciate trespassing and appreciate people taking plants from their property even less. When foraging on private land, you should ask the landowner for permission and explain what you're doing. Some people won't mind foragers, as long as you're respectful. The worst they can do is say no.

In short, if you doubt whether you can legally forage in an area, then check. Even if you're relatively sure, then check. It's the best way to stay on the right side of the law and to avoid awkward encounters or, worse, a fine.

PART TWO
THE MID-ATLANTIC
STATES WE ARE VISITING

3 DELAWARE

STATE MOTTO: "LIIBERTY AND INDEPENDENCE"

I just wanted to take a second and thank everyone for joining me on this journey. Now, let's take a walk around the area and learn a little about the topography of the places we visit in this book, starting with Delaware.

Delaware is a small state that sits on a peninsula, sharing it with Maryland and Virginia.

So, what does this mean for foragers? Knowing your area can help determine the wild edibles you can harvest. Here's a quick overview of Delaware:

- Delaware is very flat and has a low elevation. The highest point of Delaware is Ebright Azimuth, just under 450 feet above sea level. Much of Delaware is at sea level, especially along the coast.
- Delaware enjoys a moderate climate throughout the year. The monthly temperature ranges from 32 to 76°F. Near the coast, temperatures are about 10°F warmer in the winter and cooler in the summer compared to inner Delaware.
- Just over half of the days are sunny, and the stunning dune-backed beaches of Delaware border the Delaware River, Delaware Bay, and the Atlantic Ocean and are a must to visit.

Every state has areas that offer better foraging opportunities, and Delaware is no exception. It is possible to forage anywhere in rural areas. Still, we recommend heading to the Delaware Highlands or the upper Delaware River as long as you've checked the local laws. You should find a veritable bounty, including many wild edibles we will discuss in this chapter. Whether you're new to foraging or have a measure of experience, it's always a good idea to connect with local foraging groups. Here, you can find information about legal guidelines and good foraging spots, and you can even meet with some locals to go foraging together. You never know. You might find some lifelong friends in these groups.

A few of the local groups include:

- **The Delaware Highlands Mushroom Society**. If you plan on hunting fungi, going with an experienced guide is always better. It is never a good idea to eat toxic mushrooms.
- **Return to Nature.** This group, led by Dan Farella, doesn't just teach people about foraging and harvesting local wild edibles to eat. They can also help you to shore up your survival skills and develop more of an appreciation of nature. Contact them at http://returntonature.us/ for further information.

4 MARYLAND

FATTI MASCHIL, PAROLE FEMINE

Maryland...Home of Ocean City, the Ravens, the Orioles, and, of course, the blue crab.

"Maryland is such a special place, man... You miss that warm, friendly love. It ain't like that everywhere else in the world."

BENJI MADDEN, LEAD GUITARIST FOR GOOD CHARLOTTE

Maryland isn't just stunning; there are plenty of things to forage. Here's a quick overview:

- Maryland is defined mainly by the extensive waterways and coastlines of the Chesapeake Bay and the Atlantic Ocean. The main area of Maryland falls within the Atlantic Coastal Plain, bisected by the Chesapeake Bay, and divides Maryland into the Eastern and Western shores.
- Another area of Maryland is the Piedmont Plateau, which sits west of the coastal lowlands. This area has a broad, rolling upland punctuated by several deep gorges. Finally, the western extreme of Maryland is the Appalachian Mountain range, including Backbone Mountain, the highest point in Maryland at 3,360 feet above sea level.

- Maryland generally has hot, humid summers and cool winters. The western part of Maryland has harsher, longer winters and fantastic, shorter summers.

Unfortunately, it's illegal to forage in Maryland state parks. When planning a foraging trip, check the legal restrictions of that area. However, you can find good foraging spots in Bottega, Patapsco Valley, and Liberty Reservoir forests.

Local foraging groups can guide you through the area and point you toward some of the best wild edibles. Here are some groups you can connect with:

- **Forage, Maryland**. This group, a Michael Weese creation, hosts walks and foraging tours.
- **Fox Haven Organic Farm and Learning Center** in Jefferson, Md., is close to the Washington D.C. and Baltimore metro areas, giving city-dwellers a fantastic opportunity to get into foraging. They offer public and private classes on herbalism, wild food foraging, and beekeeping.
- **Maryland Mushrooms and Mycology**. Unsurprisingly, this group mainly focuses on mushrooms and fungi. They go foraging and host classes on mushroom cultivation.

Maryland is a playground of forests, waterways, and mountains. As you'd expect, it's beautiful, but these environments also offer a plethora of wild edibles to enjoy. Our exploration of the Mid-Atlantic doesn't stop in Maryland.

5 NEW JERSEY

LIBERTY AND PROSPERITY

 New Jersey is famous for a lot of things. It's one of the most multicultural areas in the United States, one of the wealthiest states, and an industrial powerhouse.

"New Jersey people, they will surprise you."

JOHN GORKA, AMERICAN FOLK MUSICIAN

However, what's relevant to us is the New Jersey landscape and whatever wonders we can forage there. Here's a quick overview of New Jersey's geography and climate.

- New Jersey sits north of Delaware and is flanked by the Delaware River and 130 miles of the Atlantic coastline. New Jersey has four distinct geographical areas, each with unique features.
- The Atlantic Coastal Plain has low hills, pine forests, and salt marshes and encompasses the sandy beaches near the coast. North of this area, you can find rolling hills and valleys.
- The western portion of New Jersey is more rugged, with flat-topped rock ridges and plenty of lakes. To the northwest, you can find the Appalachian Ridge and Valley, which includes plenty of tree-topped mountains, and the dramatic Delaware Water Gap, where the river cuts through the mountain range.

- New Jersey enjoys a relatively moderate and temperate climate, with cold winters and warm, relatively humid summers. You can expect an average range of 30°F-74°F throughout the year, but northern winters are usually more severe.

There are plenty of fantastic places to forage in New Jersey, including the Atlantic coastline and the many forests, such as the pine barrens. As in other states, make sure that you check the law before foraging in a particular area.

As before, here are some local foraging groups and classes you can contact:

- **Nathaniel Whitmore**, a local herbalist, offers wild food and medicinal herb walks in New Jersey, New York, and Pennsylvania.
- **Robin Rose Bennet** is a New Jersey and New York-based herbalist who offers classes to teach people how to use natural wild plants. **Steve Brill**, a famous forager, conducts foraging tours in the Mid-Atlantic area. He's also known as Wild Man Steve Brill.
- **Debbie Naha-Koretzky**, the Wild Edibles Lady, is a foraging instructor. She offers tours, walks, and cooking demonstrations to teach people about safe foraging practices.

6 NEW YORK

EXCELSIOR" MEANING "EVER UPWARD

New York City is a cultural powerhouse and one of the most famous cities in the United States, if not the world.

"the true New Yorker secretly believes that people living anywhere else have to be, in some sense, kidding."

JOHN UPDIKE, AMERICAN NOVELIST

Simply put, it's a fantastic place to live, and residents are in the thick of it.

However, the state of New York is more than just the city itself. Plenty of wild edibles are to be found; you must know where to look. Here's a quick overview of the state itself first:

The overall geography of this state includes a wide variety of features. You can find farms, woodlands, mountains, hilly areas, rivers, and lakes.

- New York sits on the edge of the Appalachian Mountains, where the mountains transition into hills and eventually into the lowlands surrounding Late Ontario and the St. Lawrence River.
- New York has a continental climate, with hot summers and cold winters. Temperatures can range from a minimum of 27°F to a maximum of 85°F. New York is prone to stormy weather, with plenty of rain and wind.

There are plenty of fantastic places to forage in New York. These include the city parks, much of the woods and rural areas found in the Western New York area, upstate, Catskills, and the patches of lumber in the Hudson Valley. As usual, check the rules before foraging so you don't get slapped with an unwelcome charge.

Getting involved with foraging groups is an easy way to find good foraging spots.

Steve Brill, "Wildman," is a famous foraging expert. He holds classes and tours about living off the land, including Identifying and harvesting local wild plants and mushrooms and providing delicious recipes.

7 PENNSYLVANIA
STATE MOTTO: "VIRTUE, LIBERTY AND INDEPENDENCE"

While it played a massive part in the American Industrial Revolution, Pennsylvania is still a rural state. The Northeast, forests, and Amish country are great foraging spots, offering various foraging options.

"I'm from Pennsylvania, and that love for the simplicity of life never left me."

BILL COWHER, FORMER PITTSBURGH STEELERS HEAD COACH

This amazing simplicity can be found in Pennsylvania's rural areas, which can be a pantry of wild edibles if you know where to look. Here's what you can expect from the Pennsylvanian landscape:

- As the "Keystone State," Pennsylvania bridges the Northeastern and Southern states, the Atlantic seaboard, and the Midwest. Not only that, but it also borders the Great Lakes and Canada. It spans the mid-Atlantic, Northeastern, and Appalachian regions of the United States.
- Pennsylvania is bisected by the Appalachian Mountains, which makes it a largely mountainous state. It also has valleys, plateaus, forests, streams, and large rivers.
- The only lowlands in Pennsylvania can be found in the extreme southeastern part of the state, at the Atlantic Coastal Plains.

- Pennsylvania has a humid continental climate, with an average of about 40 inches of precipitation each year and a prevailing westerly wind. There are wide fluctuations in seasonal temperatures, ranging from 28°F in January to 70°F in July.

You can usually connect with nearby foraging groups to find good places to forage and learn some trade tricks. Here are a few groups to connect with:

- **The Wild Foodies of Philly** is a volunteer group that conducts tours of wild plants in the area, showing people how to use them as food, fiber, and medicine.
- **Adam Hariton**, the well-known forager, researcher, and wild food enthusiast, offers hiking trips, outdoor activities, and presentations about foraging in Western Pennsylvania.

Wow, exploring all these areas is excellent. Is anyone tired yet? NO? Good, cause we are headed south to Virginia.

8 VIRGINIA

STATE MOTTO: "SIC SEMPER TYRANNIS"
LATIN FOR "THUS ALWAYS TYRANTS"

"The November evening had a bite; it nibbled not quite gently at her cheeks and ears. In Virginia, the late autumn was a lover, still, but a dangerous one."

J. ALEKSANDR WOOTTON, POET AND AUTHOR

Whether you plan on foraging in the fall or any other time of the year, you're sure to find some goodies as you explore the wilds of Virginia. Here's a quick overview of what you'll find in the Virginia landscape.

- Virginia sits in the mid-Atlantic and southeastern regions of the US. It stretches from the Chesapeake Bay to the Appalachian Mountain Range and has an extensive Atlantic coastline.
- The Great Valley, a gigantic trough from Quebec to Alabama, makes up Virginia's Valley and Ridge region. This enormous region contains more of the Great Valley than any other state. It features narrow and elongated

parallel ridges that reach 3000-4000 feet in height and are juxtaposed with flat, lush valleys with gently rolling hills. The effect is striking.

- The climate is generally mild, although it varies throughout the region. In southeastern Virginia and around the eastern shore, the average temperature ranges from 40°F in January to the upper 70s°F in July. In western Virginia, especially in the mountains, it can get as low as 0°F.

There are some fantastic places for people to forage in Virginia. For example, you can visit the Emerald Mountain Sanctuary, which features a guided foraging tour, Virginia Beach, Afton, Blue Ridge, and Richmond. These areas show a different side of Virginia and offer various goodies to enjoy.

The best way to find a good foraging spot is to check out some local foraging groups. Some of these can also teach you to identify specific plants and mushrooms. Here are a few groups that you can connect with:

- **Eco Images**, founded by Vickie Shafer, offers classes in Virginia Beach to teach people how to explore the outdoors, forage safely, and use whatever they find as food or medicine.
- **Julie Carestio Pettler**, a local herbalist based in Frederick County, offers classes, foraging trips, and workshops to teach people how to make medicine.
- **The Earth Connection School**, founded by Tim MacWelch, is located in Somerville. It's an outdoor school that focuses on wild foods and survival skills.
- **Tracks and Roots**, created by Alison Meehan, is located in Richmond. Alison, along with other instructors, offers wilderness survival and foraging courses.

9 WEST VIRGINIA

STATE MOTTO: "MONTANI SEMPER LIBERI" LATIN FOR "MOUNTAINEERS ARE ALWAYS FREE."

West Virginia is a beautiful place to live, and, as usual, you can find plenty of goodies to forage as long as you know where to look.

"the sun doesn't always shine in West Virginia, but the people do."

RICHARD OJEDA, FORMER WEST VIRGINIA CONGRESSMAN

As with other states, West Virginia is made up of different regions and has a unique geography that informs what grows there and where you can find wild edibles.

- West Virginia borders five different states. It's east of Ohio and Kentucky, south of Pennsylvania, west of Maryland, and, predictably, west of Virginia.
- West Virginia can be split into three different regions. The west and north encompass the Allegheny plateau. The
- Allegheny mountains run from the southwest of West Virginia to the Northeast. Finally, the Ridge and Valley areas sit along the border between Virginia and West Virginia. The landscape includes the eastern panhandle, the Great Appalachian Valley, and the Blue Ridge Mountains.
- The climate of West Virginia includes hot, humid summers, mild, crisp winters, and moderate precipitation throughout the year. The temperature

rarely tops 90°F in the summer, and residents usually experience snow in winter.

There are plenty of great places to forage in West Virginia, such as the mountainous areas. Monongahela National Forest is a popular spot for foragers. You can also explore the wooded areas in southern West Virginia.

As always, please check out the local guidelines and restrictions for foraging in this state, but the good news is that West Virginia is especially forager-friendly.

Getting involved in a local foraging group is a great way to discover new foraging spots and learn more about identifying wild plants in West Virginia. Here are a couple to try:

- **Mountaineer Wilderness LLC**, founded by Mark Chapin, is based in Canaan Valley. The classes and courses focus on survival skills and getting the most out of the wilderness.
- **The West Virginia Mushroom Club** is a non-profit organization located in Charleston. As you'd expect, it focuses on educating people about mushrooms.
- **The Living Earth School** is based in the Blue Ridge Mountains. The organization aims to develop naturalist and survival skills, such as camping and foraging.

Shew, that was a long walk; does everyone get their steps in? Let's take a load off and jump right into the part of the book that you've been waiting for. Starting with something sweet...Fruits and Shrubs.

NOTE FROM THE PUBLISHER

We completely understand the advantages of using color photos to identify plants. However, to make this book edition more affordable, we decided to use black-and-white photographs, which helped us reduce printing costs, and we passed that savings on to you. But don't worry—we have a solution for you! Scan the QR code below and download a complimentary printable PDF file that includes vibrant, clear, color photos of all the plants featured in the book. Happy Foraging!

PART THREE
FRUITS AND SHRUBS

A

llegheny Blackberry

Rubus allegheniensis [ROO-bus al-leh-gay-nee-en-sis]

The Allegheny Blackberry is a part of the *Rosaceae* (rose) family. They are found throughout North America. Blackberry bush growth is increased after a natural disaster such as a fire but will die back after the tree seedlings it protects start to take root and grow.

You can find blackberries at the edges of wooded areas, gardens, wastelands, roadways, fields, and meadows.

Identification:

Growth/Size: A deciduous, native shrub that grows in a tangle of canes up to 8 feet tall and 10 feet wide.

Bark/Stem/Root: These stems are brown or reddish brown with stout prickles that are straight or slightly curved. The tips are green where there's new growth.

Leaf: There are usually three or *palmately compound* leaves with long *petioles*. Each leaflet is up to 4 inches long and 3 inches wide, generally twice as long as broad. There are usually two serrated margins on an *ovate* leaflet. The leaves will change to Red, orange, or purple in the fall before dropping their leaves for winter.

FLOWER: Five-petaled white flowers appear in loose terminal clusters from May to June. *Racemes* of about 12 white flowers appear on the canes. No floral scent is present.

FRUIT/SEED/NUT: July is fruit season. Depending on moisture levels, *aggregate drupes* are around 3/4 inch long and 1/3 inch wide in the summer. Initially, the *drupes* are white or green, then red, then black. They're seedy and sweet when fully ripened. The fruit should come off the stem clean, revealing a solid, fleshy core.

Look-a-likes: They can sometimes be mistaken for black raspberries, which are also edible. Several other members of the Rubus genus are similar as well.

Cautions: Take care when harvesting blackberries, and wear long sleeves; the thorns can be nasty.

Culinary Uses: You can eat blackberries raw as you are harvesting or with a sprinkling of sugar once home for a tad of extra sweetness. They also work very well when baked into a pie or turned into jam.

Medicinal Uses: The roots are anti-hemorrhoidal, anti-rheumatic, *astringent*, stimulant, and tonic. An infusion can treat stomach complaints, diarrhea, piles, coughs and colds, tuberculosis, and rheumatism. The infusion has also been used by women threatened with a miscarriage. Infusions of the root can be used to soothe sore eyes. The leaves are astringent. An infusion can be used in the treatment of diarrhea. Urinary problems have been treated with an infusion of the bark. A decoction of the stems has been used as a diuretic.

Fun/Historical Fact: In the UK, some believe blackberries should not be harvested after October 11th (Old Michaelmas Day). They think that after this day, the devil will spit, step, or foul the berries, making them unfit to eat. Because October is cool, humid, and often wet, a bacteria called Botryotinia can invade the berries, causing them to go rancid and causing illness.

Pet Toxicity: Not toxic to your furry friends.

A utumn Olive

Elaeagnus umbellata [EL-EE-AG-NUS UM-BELL-AY-TUH]

Back in the early 1800s, a plant emerged on the scene, bringing many benefits. It played a crucial role in providing habitats for wildlife, combating erosion, and transforming wastelands into fertile grounds. Known as Elaeagnus, Oleaster, or the captivating Japanese silverberry, this plant belongs to the Elaeagnaceae family.

With its remarkable resilience, Autumn Olive can thrive in almost any location. Whether it's disturbed ground, roadside areas, forest perimeters, or serene meadows, this hardy plant can be found adding its vibrant presence to these diverse landscapes.

Identification:

GROWTH/SIZE: Deciduous tree/shrub with a rapid growth rate that can grow up to 20 feet tall.

BARK/STEM/ROOT: Split, furrowed, dark gray bark with dense scale coverings. The bark peels off in long, narrow strips as the plant ages.

LEAF: There are **alternate** dark green leaves (young leaves have silvery scales) with entire but wavy margins. On their upper side, they're dull green, while the underside has brown scales. The leaf length is 2-4 inches, and the width is half that.

29

FLOWER: The flowers bloom from late spring to early summer. They are showy and fragrant, borne in clusters of 1-7 in the leaf axils. Keep an eye on the number of flowers one bush has in the spring for an indication of how your fall berry harvest will be.

FRUIT/SEED/NUT: The fruits resemble olives in size, with a vibrant red color with shimmering silver or brown scales when fully ripe. Measuring around 1/3 to 1/4 inches long once mature, the ripe berries effortlessly detach from the plant, but it's advisable to wait a few days if there are any remaining orange berries. Although harvesting can start in September, they become even sweeter if you can exercise patience and wait until after the first frost.

Look-a-likes: Two shrubs resemble Autumn olive, but both have opposite leaves: Silver buffalo-berry (Shepherdia argentea), which is non-native, and the native Russet buffalo-berry (S. canadensis), which has brown-scaly young twigs and undersides of leaves.

Caution: The only hazard is the sharp thorns, so while picking your fantastic fruit, beware not to get pricked.

Culinary Uses: You can eat fresh, raw autumn olives, but many people process them to take full advantage of their sour flavor. Most recipes involve creating a thick puree by boiling 8 cups of berries with 1 cup of water for 20 minutes, then stirring, mashing, and straining to remove the seeds and stems. You can use this puree in baking recipes, jams, smoothies, sauces, and dehydrated fruit rolls.

Medicinal Uses: The Autumn Olive, also known as the Invasive Super-berry, is a fantastic source of Lycopene. Let's compare the numbers, shall we? A cup of tomatoes contains 4.6mg of Lycopene, but when you cook them, that level skyrockets to around 26mg per cup. An Autumn Olive contains a whopping 38mg of Lycopene in just 100mg of raw fruit!

Fun/Historical Fact: Autumn Olive is an invasive species that grows throughout the Mid-Atlantic region. It chokes out native plants, but you can help reduce its spread by picking the berries and enjoying them yourself.

Pet Toxicity: Not toxic to your furry friends.

B each Plum
Prunus maritima [PROO-nus muh-RIT-ih-muh]

These juicy, tart fruits are a popular foraging option for anyone near the beach. Just make sure you get there before the birds. Plum Island, New York, and Beach Plum Island State Park in Sussex County, Delaware, are named after Beach Plums, a *Rosaceae* (rose) family member. Some familiar names are seaside plum, sand plum, Graves' plum, Shore plum, Graves' beach plum, and American plum.

As the name suggests, beach plums are found in sandy soil near the shore, among the dunes, and on the coastal plans.

Identification:

GROWTH/SIZE: It usually grows in a low spreading manner to form dense thickets up to 8 feet tall but has been known to reach heights of up to 18 feet.

BARK/STEM/ROOT: A beach plum's immature bark is reddish brown and smooth with horizontal bands of *lenticels*. The bark darkens and gets rougher as the shrub ages. New growth and young twigs are also reddish browns.

LEAF: When mature, the dark green glossy leaves are velvety or hairy on the underside. They're *alternate*ly arranged, finely toothed, *egg-shaped*, and measure 0.75-2.75 inches long and half that wide.

31

FLOWER: In April or May, before leaf-out, small **umbel**-like clusters of two to three white flowers bloom and last until June. The five-petalled flowers measure 0.5 inches across and have long *filaments* and yellow **anthers**. They have hairy stalks and *sepals*.

FRUIT/SEED/NUT: The fruit is a bluish-purple to deep purple. Although less common, it can also be dark red or yellow. This cherry-shaped edible fruit has a 0.5-1 inch diameter and ripens from August to September. The fruit's flavor can range from naturally sweet to tart or bitter. They're drupes with one **egg-shaped**, stone-like seed inside.

Look-a-likes: The fruit resembles a grape, but they have stones like other plums. The plants also look like beach roses, but those fruits are red.

Caution: In most places, the bush is accompanied by poison ivy intertwined throughout.

Culinary Uses: Though the plums can be eaten raw, they are usually quite tart. Most harvest the plums to make jellies and jams. (See recipe section for instructions)

Medicinal Uses: The vitamin C in this fruit boosts the body's immune reaction and counters the common cold and flu. *Phenolic compounds* and **flavonoids** in the fruit have an anti-inflammatory effect and help to fight obesity at a cellular level. In addition, many of the issues caused by obesity are decreased, like heart diseases, diabetes, or high cholesterol levels.

Fun/Historical Facts: Beach plums make a great additive to alcohol. Here are a winery and a distillery making great use of their local harvest. **Natali Vineyards** in Goshen, New Jersey, and **Beach Time Distilling** in Lewes, Delaware, use plums to make different alcoholic beverages. If you are a brewer or distiller with leftovers from your harvest, try it and see what you can develop.

Pet Toxicity: The plum itself is not toxic, but the seed and the plant contain cyanide, which can be deadly to your furry friends.

Bearberry

Arctostaphylos uva-ursi [ARK-TOH-STAF-ih-LOHS YOO-va UR-SEE]

The Bearberry got its name due to being a favorite snack for...you guessed it... BEARS! The Bearberry is a part of the *Ericaceae* (heath) family. They are commonly known as Mountain Blueberry, Southern Mountain Cranberry, Bearberry, Arando, or Dingleberry. The other common name for the Bearberry is a Kinnikinnick. Kinnikinnick is the Algonquian Indian word for a mixture.

These plants grow in sandy and rocky areas. They are along shorelines, hillsides, and mixed or coniferous forests.

Identification:

GROWTH/SIZE: dense shrub with high salt spray and drought tolerance. It grows up to 6 feet wide but only gets 1 foot tall.

BARK/STEM/ROOT: papery, reddish bark.

LEAF: 1-inch, leathery, dark green leaves that are teardrop-shaped. The colors change from yellow to green in the spring to dark green in the summer and bronze to reddish-purple in the winter.

FLOWER: Clusters of small, five-petaled white-pink flowers bloom from April and last into fall.

Fruit/Seed/Nut: Bright red berries follow the flowers. They are 1/4 to 1/2 inch green fruits that turn red in the fall and persist into winter.

Look-a-likes: They look similar to cranberries or lingonberries, but both are edible. However, ensure you can correctly identify any berry like this before eating.

Caution: When consuming large quantities, nausea or stomach upset may occur.

Culinary Uses: These berries aren't great raw, but you can cook them to bring out their natural, cranberry-like sweetness. Otherwise, use the young leaves to make tea.

Medicinal Uses: Among the best antiseptics for treating urinary infections, bearberry helps reduce bacteria in the urine. It helps treat urinary tract infections (UTI) and *urolithiasis* and reduces inflammation.

If you are prone to headaches, you'll appreciate this next one. In traditional medicine, bearberry has been used to relieve headaches for hundreds of years. To achieve this benefit, dry the leaves of the uva-ursi shrub and then smoke them. Dried Bearberry leaves will produce a similar effect to the cannabis plant.

Fun/Historical Fact: The Algonquian Indians used the leaves and tobacco leaves during religious ceremonies. Combinations of these two types of leaves were made in two ways. They created a Smudge stick, burned it to deter evil spirits, or smoked it in the ceremonial pipe, hoping the smoker's dreams would be carried to the Great Spirit.

Pet Toxicity: The berries themselves are not toxic, but the seed inside and the plant contain cyanide, which can be deadly to your furry friends.

Black Elderberry

Sambucus canadensis [SAM-BOO-KUS KAN-AH-DEN-SIS]

There are two types of elderberries in the Mid-Atlantic region. The most common is the black elderberry. Still, you can find red elderberries in some parts of the state. It is a member of the *Adoxaceae* (muskroot) family. Common names are American Elder, American Elderberry, and Common Elderberry.

Elderberries like moist soil. You can find them along roadsides, trails, fences, and forests. They also grow in swamps and wasteland.

Identification:

GROWTH/SIZE: This tree is native to North America and is a woody, **deciduous** shrub or small tree that grows from 5 to 12 feet tall and 6 to 10 feet wide.

BARK/STEM/ROOT: Short **lenticels** on the bark give it a warty appearance. The bark is yellowish gray to light grayish brown. A young woody branch has scattered **lenticels** that are light grayish brown. Shoots are pale green when young, and the **pith** is white.

LEAF: The leaves are bright green and have 5 to 11 leaflets, but most have 7. They are **oval** to **lance-shaped,** measuring 2 to 6 inches long and 0.5 to 2.5 inches wide. There's a wedge-shaped base with an abruptly narrow tip. In the fall, the foliage turns yellow.

FLOWER: During June, creamy-white fragrant flowers with six petals shaped like a star appear in flat-topped or rounded clusters between 4 and 10 inches.

FRUIT/SEED/NUT: Clusters of rounded, edible, purple-black **drupes**. The berries measure 1/4 inch across, have 3-5 seeds, and are in bulky clusters.

Look-a-likes: There are two plants, Pokeweed (*phytolacca americana*), a plant that produces larger berries that hang in a long cylinder, and the Devil's Walking Stick (*Aralia spinosa*); berries are similar in appearance to elderberries, but the main stem has large thorns.

Caution: Remember that elder stems, leaves, and unripe berries are toxic and should not be consumed. Only the flowers and ripe berries are edible; the berries need to be cooked before eating. All parts of the plant contain **cyanogenic glycosides,** which are metabolized into cyanide when consumed. Cooking helps destroy the compounds, making them harmless. Some mild symptoms include nausea, vomiting, and diarrhea. Elderberries can lead to coma and death if not prepared properly.

Culinary Uses: Elderflowers can be used to make cordial or wine. The berries make a great addition to fruit pies, jams, or jellies.

Medicinal Uses: This berry is helpful for colds, touches of flu, and H1N1 "swine" flu. Additionally, it boosts your immune system and is used for HIV/AIDS. You can also use elderberry for sinus pain, back and leg pain (sciatica), nerve pain (neuropathy), and chronic fatigue syndrome (CFS).

Besides treating hay fever (allergic rhinitis) and cancer, elderberries are used as laxatives, diuretics, and sweat inducers. It can also combat heart disease, high cholesterol, headaches, toothaches, and weight loss.

Fun/Historical Fact: These plants can self-pollinate, but flies are their primary pollination source.

Pet Toxicity: the leaves, stems, unripe fruit, and root are poisonous to dogs as they contain cyanide, even in small quantities.

N orthern Highbush Blueberry

Vaccinium corymbosum [vak-SIN-ee-um coh-rim-BOH-sum]

Blueberries are deliciously sweet, easy to identify, and unarmed with thorns or prickles, making them an excellent fruit for novice foragers. They look similar to commercial blueberries but are smaller and have a more intense flavor. Highbush blueberry is in the *Ericaceae* (heath) family and is native to eastern North America.

Most wild blueberries prefer acidic soil and can be found in woods, thickets, and rocky areas. You might also find them near swamps.

Identification:

GROWTH/SIZE: An upright *deciduous* shrub with oddly shaped branches forming a rounded, compact outline, usually growing 6-12 ft. high and wide.

BARK/STEM/ROOT: The bark on old stems is gray-brown and thinly furrowed. New shoots are glabrous and yellowish-green to reddish.

LEAF: An *ovate*, reddish-green spring leaf turns blue-green in summer with lighter undersides. This plant has beautiful fall colors: red, yellow, orange, and purple.

FLOWER: Tiny pink or white bell-shaped flowers mature in clusters from March to May.

Fruit/Seed/Nut: Blue to purple small 1-inch round fruits with a 5-pointed crown begin to ripen from a green to pink color to full blue ripeness in August. Once fully ripe, they detach easily from their stems.

Look-a-likes: Being a part of the same genus, the Huckleberry (Vaccinium ovatum) resembles the blueberry, but in coastal regions, the berries will have a reddish tinge, and in the mountains, the berries will be dark blue.

Wintergreen (Gaultheria procumbens): the round berries have a dusky red color and resemble the red-berried variety of blueberries but have the minty taste of wintergreen.

Caution: Some toxic dark berries can be mistaken for blueberries, but you should be okay if you look for the 5-pointed crown on the end.

Culinary Uses: You can eat raw blueberries or freeze them for future use. You can also preserve blueberries by drying them or canning them in syrup. Blueberry pancakes or muffins are a firm favorite for many families.

Medicinal Uses: Blueberries are rich in *phenolic compounds* and *anthocyanins*. They have been demonstrated to have certain health benefits, including improved cognition, reduced cardiovascular concerns, and cancer risk. The blueberry is the only known plant with an actual blue color. *Anthocyanin,* the pigment in blueberries that gives them color, is also responsible for this fantastic fruit's great nutritional benefits. Compared to 40 different fruits, the blueberry is ranked number 1 in antioxidant health benefits and only has 44 calories per 1/2 cup.

Fun Facts: North American indigenous people called Blueberries "star-fruits" because the end of the berry has a five-pointed star shape.

Pet Toxicity: Non-toxic to your pup.

Chickasaw Plum

Prunus angustifolia [PROO-nus an-gus-tee-FOH-lee-uh]

Chickasaw plums are consistently sweet, which makes them an excellent option for foragers. They're one of three plum species native and familiar to the United States. It is a part of the **Rosaceae** (rose) family. Other common names for these outstandingly hardy plants are Sandhill plum, mountain cherry, and sand plum.

Chickasaw trees and thickets can be found along trails, roads, and fences and in open areas like scrub forest clearings, meadows, and prairies. They like sandy soil.

Identification:

GROWTH/SIZE: The native, deciduous tree usually grows about 15 feet tall and can be as wide as 20 feet.

BARK/STEM/ROOT: It has red, smooth bark with many elongated, light **lenticels**. The tree bark gets scaly and shallowly furrowed as it ages. Reddish-brown branches and twigs sometimes have thorny lateral branches.

Leaf: It has **alternate** leaves with finely toothed margins.

FLOWER: A clump of 5-petaled, white flowers that mature from March to April.

FRUIT/SEED/NUT: The **drupes** mature to about 1/2 inch long and yellow-to-red from May to July.

Look-a-likes: The flatwood plum tree looks similar but tends to grow alone. Flatwood plums produce black or yellow plums that can be very hard and bitter, edible but unpalatable.

Caution: The fruit itself is not toxic, but the leaves, stems, and the pit or seed of the fruit all contain substances that break down into hydrocyanic acid (cyanide).

Culinary Uses: These plums are delicious, but you can use them for jelly, pies, preserves, wine, and other sweet treats.

Medicinal Uses: Although this species is not explicitly mentioned, all members of the genus contain *amygdalin and prunasin,* substances that, when broken down, produce *hydrocyanic acid* (cyanide). It's highly poisonous, but in small doses, it stimulates breathing, improves digestion, and gives you energy.

Fun/Historical Fact: The Chickasaw Plum comes from a tree initially cultivated by the Chickasaw tribe in 1874. The tribe used fresh fruit to produce jams, jellies, and wine. They also dried the fruit for winter consumption.

Pet Toxicity: This fruit is the same for pups and their humans. The fruit is not toxic; the pit or seed can kill your furry friends.

D og Rose

Rosa canina [RO-SA CAN-INA]

Roses aren't just beautiful. Some roses produce fruits called rosehips. Rosehips are the bulbous area under the flower itself. They are called the fruit of the rose and come in striking colors such as red to orange, and you can even find black or yellow varieties. They are easily found in the wild and belong to the **Rosaceae** (rose) family. Other common names are Brier Hip, Dog Brier, Dog Rose Fruit, Hip Berries, Witches Brier, and Hip Rose. Several types of roses produce rosehips.

Roses are an excellent beginner forage; they are well-known and easily spotted. Wild roses can be found in fields, scrub, and disturbed areas along roadsides, hiking trails, and woodland edges.

Identification:

GROWTH/SIZE: the plant is a shrub and proliferates to 9 feet.

BARK / STEM / ROOT: this shrub has sharp, stout, curving thorns.

LEAF: There are 5–7 leaflets on its *pinnate* leaves with teeth lining the edge of the leaf blade. When bruised, the leaves smell amazing. As the weather gets colder, the leaves drop.

FLOWER: The flowers are usually pale pink but can also be deep pink or white. They bloom from June to July. Each flower has five petals and measures approximately 1.6-2.4 inches. When the *sepals* are viewed from underneath, two are whiskered (or bearded) on both sides, two are smooth, and one has a whisker (or beard) on just one side.

FRUIT/SEED/NUT: the rosehips ripen from October to December and tend to be sweeter after the first frost.

Look-a-likes: Several wild rose species can be found while foraging. Wild strawberries, hawthorn, and crab apple are other wildflowers in the rose family. Briars, brambles, raspberries, and cloudberries are all close relatives you will likely find on your journey.

Caution: As with other thorny plants, avoid getting injured while harvesting the fruit. Below the fruit's flesh is a layer of hair around the seeds. If you eat them, they can irritate your mouth and digestive tract.

Culinary Uses: Rosehips can be made into syrup as a great way to add more vitamin C to your diet. You can make jams, jellies, and pies or use them to make tea or wine. Check out these varieties for your best shot at finding your prize. Dog Rose (Rosa canina), Rugosa Rose (Rosa rugosa), Prickly Wild Rose (Rosa acicularis), and Cinnamon Rose (Rosa cinnamomea). The wild dog rose is considered the best rosehip source.

Medicinal Uses: They're a brilliant source of vitamin C, up to 20 times more than oranges. Rosehips contain Lycopene and carotene, like carrots. Therefore, it makes sense that they would benefit the skin and eyes.

Fun/Historical Fact: Rosehips have gained plenty of notoriety in the beauty and healthcare industries. Rosehip oil has been used for years to delay the signs of aging, though there is little scientific proof.

Pet Toxicity: You don't have to worry about your dog getting sick from roses. Their flowers, petals, and rose hips are non-toxic.

Hardy Kiwi
Actinidia arguta [AC-TINI-DIA ARGUTA]

The Hardy kiwi is a little-known fruit native to Asia that grows readily in the Northern United States. It is considered a super fruit as it is incredibly nutritious. It is a part of the ***Actinidiaceae*** family. It has several aliases Siberian gooseberry, Siberian Kiwi, kiwi berry, arctic Kiwi, baby kiwi, dessert kiwi, grape kiwi, northern Kiwi, or cocktail kiwi.

Invasive hardy kiwis can be found in wooded areas. Since the vines are fast-growing, they can prosper in any situation as long as a male and a female plant are present for pollination.

Identification:

GROWTH/SIZE: Typically grown for its pretty foliage and edible fruit. The vine grows to 25-30' or more but can climb as much as 100' into trees in its native habitat.

BARK / STEM / ROOT: It's a deciduous, fast-growing, twining woody vine.

LEAF: Spring brings broad-*ovate* to *elliptic* deep green leaves 3-5 inches long.

FLOWER: Flowering in June, this greenish-white flower is 3/4 inches long.

FRUIT/SEED/NUT: Smooth-skinned grape-sized fruits 1 1/4 inches long mature in

September-October. Hardy kiwifruit is sweeter than kiwifruit and doesn't have to be peeled, so they can be eaten whole.

Look-a-likes: Hardy kiwi is grown commercially, so ensure you haven't stumbled upon private property when harvesting.

Caution: In people allergic to Kiwi, it can cause allergic reactions such as trouble swallowing (dysphagia), vomiting, and hives. Kiwis may also reduce blood clotting and increase bleeding.

Culinary Uses: Unlike its cousin, the Kiwi we all know and love, the Hardy Kiwi has smooth skin and does not need to be peeled to be eaten. The Kiwi is best when they're perfectly ripe and soft, but you can pick them underripe and let them ripen at home. There is a debate on the actual taste; the list of comparisons gets more significant by the day. Some fuzzy Kiwi, strawberry, pineapple, and banana flavors have all been reported depending on the variety.

Medicinal Uses: none known

Fun/Historical Fact: In Korea, Hardy Kiwi is known as darae. Young leaves, called darae-sun, are often consumed as a namul vegetable. Namul refers to a variety of edible grass or leaves. Wild greens are called san-namul, meaning "mountain namul," and spring vegetables are called bom-namul, meaning "spring namul." On the day of Daeboreum, the first full moon of the year, Koreans eat boreum-namul, meaning "full moon namul," with five-grain rice. It's believed that boreum namuls consumed in winter help one to withstand the heat of the summer to come.

Pet Toxicity: Dogs can benefit from hardy kiwi's nutrients. Boost your dog's immunity with hardy kiwis, which have antioxidants and vitamin C. The fruit also has calcium, fiber, potassium, and lutein. Dogs should eat it in moderation, though, as the fruit contains oxalic acid that can irritate their throats.

J apanese Barberry

Berberis thunbergii [BER-BER-IS THUN-BER-JEE-EYE]

Japanese barberry is an exotic, widespread, and invasive plant cultivated initially for decorative purposes in the 1860s and is native to China and Japan. They produce edible leaves and tart berries. You can also use the inner bark of the roots as a crude antibiotic. You can find native barberry species in the wild, but the Japanese variety is more common.

Barberry can be found in dense forests and other shady areas. It's familiar enough that you may find it in different habitats, like parks, gardens, and forest edges.

Identification:

GROWTH/SIZE: This is a ***deciduous***, invasive shrub that can grow from 3 to 7 feet in height and is usually broader than tall if kept unpruned.

BARK/STEM/ROOT: The shrub's stems are covered in sharp thorns, making them painful to handle without leather gloves.

LEAF: Leaves are sparse, oval, or spatulated, 1/2 inch long and 1/8 inch wide, ranging from green to blue-green (reddish or purple in some cultivars).

FLOWER: Late spring (April to May) is when this plant blooms with 0.5-inch pale yellow flowers often hidden under leaves. Droopy ***inflorescences*** have a sub*umbel*-

late arrangement, are grouped in two to five sets, are weakly fetid, and have *pedicels* and *racemes*.

FRUIT/SEED/NUT: These plants produce bright red, glossy berries about 1/3 to 1 inch long in the fall. This ellipsoidal berry sticks around for harvesting through the winter.

Look-a-likes: There are no authentic look-a-likes.

Caution: This plant has plenty of sharp thorns, so take care.

Culinary Uses: The berries are commonly eaten, but the leaves can be cooked and eaten. They are bitter, tart, and slightly sweet. You can use them in fruit pies, jelly preserves, and drinks.

Look-a-likes: American barberry (Berberis canadensis), Common or European barberry (Berberis vulgaris), and other deciduous Berberis species are sometimes confused with this species; they are most easily distinguished by the flowers being in *umbels* and not *racemes*.

Medicinal Uses: Barberry berries have been used in traditional medicine for centuries to treat digestive issues, infections, and skin conditions because they contain anthocyanin and berbine. Anthocyanins are believed to have anti-inflammatory, antimicrobial, anticancer, and anti-obesity properties and can prevent cardiovascular disease. Berbine acts like a powerful antioxidant and may help in the fight against high blood sugar and high cholesterol levels. It may also help slow the progression of certain cancer cells, fight infections, and have anti-inflammatory effects.

Fun/Historical Fact: In 1875, the Japanese barberry was introduced to the US as an ornamental plant. Those seeds came from Russia to the Arnold Arboretum in Boston. It was planted in the New York Botanical Garden in 1896. Later, it was promoted as a replacement for Berberis vulgaris, an exotic plant introduced by European settlers. The shrub was used for hedgerows, dyes, and jams and was found to be a host for black stem rust in wheat.

Pet Toxicity: The entire plant is toxic for your pup, but worse yet, the barberry is a sanctuary for ticks, increasing the risk of Lyme disease.

N annyberry
Viburnum lentago [VIH-BUR-NUM LENT-AH-GO]

Besides its compact habit and lustrous foliage, it has beautiful and abundant flowers, handsome edible fruit, and gorgeous autumn color. Nannyberry, also known as Viburnum, Cowberry, Sweet Berry, Sheep berry, and Black Haw, is a part of the **Adoxaceae** (muskroot) family. It's sweet and has an exciting flavor similar to a combination of banana and prune.

Viburnum is commonly found in moist areas with rich loam to clay-loam soil, such as low woods, swamp borders, or near stream banks are familiar places to see it, but it tolerates dry locations too.

Identification:

GROWTH/SIZE: Viburnum bushes are dense, growing 8 to 15 feet in diameter and 15-18 feet tall when mature.

BARK/STEM/ROOT: It's brown and smooth on the stems and young branches, and there are small, dark gray to black patches on the bark.

LEAF: The leaves are simple, broad, and very finely toothed ranging from dark green in the spring to red or maroon in the fall.

FLOWER: The white flowers grow in massive, dramatic clusters. The flowers range from white/cream to blue/black and are atop a 3 to 4-inch flat-topped cyme. Individual flowers are 1/4-inch across with five petals and long stamens.

FRUIT/SEED/NUT: The fruit is a mixture of 1/2-inch light green, pale yellow, and red-pink fruits in the same cluster, slowly changing to blue-black.

Look-a-likes: Some similar edible fruits, like the sweet haw, which is almost identical to viburnum, and Northern Wild Raisin, which are smaller and taste like raisins. Some toxic purple-black fruits ripen simultaneously, like buckthorn, but they don't look that similar.

Caution: plant allergies are always a chance when harvesting something new. Though no known cautions exist for these little beauties, always use common sense while foraging.

Culinary Uses: You can eat viburnum raw. Many people prefer to process them and make a puree, separating the seeds. You can then use the puree in baking or eat it.

Medicinal Uses: Nannyberry has been used as a diuretic to relieve fluid retention and treat diarrhea, spasms, and asthma. Female uses for Nannyberry are menstrual cramps, uterus spasms resulting from childbirth, and miscarriage prevention.

Fun/Historical Fact: The common name comes from nanny goats eating ripe berries.

Pet Toxicity: Not toxic to your furry friends.

Northern Spicebush

Lindera benzoin [LIN-DER-ah BEN-zo-een]

The spicebush is a native shrub that is part of the **Lauracaea** (laurel) family and is sometimes considered ornamental, as the flowers, leaves, and berries are beautiful. But the berries can also act as a fantastic and complex spice to add something special to sweet and savory food.

It prefers shady areas, and you'll often find it under hardwood trees like beeches, oaks, and maples.

Identification:

GROWTH/SIZE: The spicebush grows 8-15 feet tall and is deciduous and a native plant of North America.

BARK/STEM/ROOT: The stem has a flat bark covered with small, circular **lenticels** that give it a rough texture. This bark has a fragrant aroma, is astringent, and tastes pleasant.

LEAF: This plant has thick, *alternate, oblong-obovate*, light green leaves up to 5 inches long, which turn yellow in autumn. Crunching the leaves releases a spicy scent.

FLOWER: In early spring, before the foliage emerges (March-April), spicebush branches are covered in greenish-yellow flowers with an aromatic scent.

FRUIT/SEED/NUT: The fruit is a red, ***ellipsoidal drupe*** roughly 1/2 inch long. It contains a large seed with a "turpentine-like" flavor and smell. The berries turn red in the fall and remain on the plant, ready to harvest, for a few months.

Look-a-likes: There are a few, but none are toxic. Even so, only harvest spicebush if you know what it is.

Cautions: plant allergies are always a chance when harvesting something new. Though no known cautions exist for these little beauties, always use common sense while foraging.

Culinary Uses: The leaves can be turned into a mild tea. The berries are spicy and slightly floral, like allspice mixed with black pepper. You can use them fresh or dehydrate them. Use them as spices, either whole or ground.

Medicinal Info/Uses: There are a lot of uses for spicebush as a household remedy, especially for colds, dysentery, and intestinal parasites. In the past, the oil from the fruits was used to treat bruises and rheumatism. A steam bath made from twigs helps ease aches and pains by raising your body's temperature and making you sweat. There was once a popular remedy for typhoid fever using the bark.

Fun/Historical Fact: This plant is called the "forsythia of the wilds" because its early spring flowering gives lowland woods a subtle yellow tinge.

Pet Toxicity: Not enough information for a definite Yes or No on this one. I would avoid it if possible since other shrubs in the Laurel family are known to be poisonous to your pup.

Asimina triloba [AH-SIH-MIN-AH TRIH-LO-BAH]

Pawpaws are a deliciously sweet fruit with a tropical flavor reminiscent of bananas and mangos. It's hard to find in stores because it's so soft and spoils quickly, so you have to either find it in farmer's markets or, more likely, forage it yourself.

Pawpaws grow in clusters in shady, wooded areas near rivers and streams.

Identification:

GROWTH/SIZE: A native, deciduous medium-growth tree that can exceed 30 feet tall and stretch just as wide.

BARK/STEM/ROOT: When they're young, there's a cinnamon-brown color to the buds and stems. Wart-like **lenticels** are spattered throughout the smooth, brown surface, and the bark becomes fissured and scaly as it ages.

LEAF: The leaves are alternate, obovate to oblong, 6-12 inches long, and 2-3 inches wide, and they smell like green peppers when crushed. The underside is pale and glaucous.

FLOWER: Monoecious flowers with six petals 1 to 1.5 inches bloom from March to May.

Fruit/Seed/Nut: Has a dull grayish-green or blue color, and the flesh becomes soft and custard-like, and it has a sweet taste like bananas. It's very nutritious and is ready for harvest from August to October. For this plant to set fruit, it needs a pollinator plant. The fruit will not ripen after it's harvested, so you can't harvest it early.

Look-a-likes: You can shake the tree to help ripe fruits along but wear a hard hat. They can fall quite unpredictably.

Caution: Gloves are recommended when harvesting since contact dermatitis can happen. Eating the fruit's skin or seeds can give you stomach and intestinal pain.

Culinary Uses: You can eat the custard or turn it into ice cream. Pawpaw can replace bananas in baking recipes for a tropical twist. You must use Pawpaws quickly because they bruise easily and spoil within days.

Medicinal Info/Uses: Every part of the pawpaw plant can be used homeopathically to treat illnesses. Laxative properties can be found in the fruit. Leaves from the plant can be infused in tea as a diuretic and applied externally to boils, ulcers, and abscesses. The seed contains alkaline asiminine, which can cause vomiting or act as a narcotic. They have also been powdered and applied to hair to kill lice. The bark is a bitter tonic. It contains alkaline analobine, which is used medicinally.

Fun/Historical Fact: Pawpaws are easy to spot in spring, as the distinctive, purplish-red flowers bloom before the leaves, standing out.

The Shawnee tribe was known to have a special connection to this fruit. Their calendar featured a month dedicated to pawpaws, called "asimi." The Lenape and Powhatan tribes also ate the fruit raw and mashed it into dried cakes to be eaten later.

Pet Toxicity: Not toxic to your furry friends, but if eaten in large quantities, it may cause diarrhea.

Persimmon
Diospyros virginiana [DY-OS-PE-RES VER-JIN-EE-AY-NAH]

Persimmons are a delicious forager's treat. They're delightful as long as they're fully ripe. American persimmon, eastern persimmon, possumwood, possum apples, and sugar plum are other names. It is a member of the *Ebenaceae* (ebony) family.

Persimmons grow in full or partial sun and can be found on sandy soils, such as on the dunes near the coast. Most other plants struggle in this soil.

Identification:

GROWTH/SIZE: persimmon is a woody, deciduous, slow-growing tree native to the Eastern and Central United States. They can grow up to 80 feet tall and be 35 feet wide.

BARK/STEM/ROOT: Its thick, dark gray bark is divided by furrows into square blocks. It's sometimes called "alligator bark" due to the resemblance to the skin on the alligator's back.

LEAF: They have broad, oblong, pointed leaves, smooth edges, or some serrations. A rounded base and an acuminate apex make them 2 to 6 inches long and 2 to 3 inches wide. Young leaves may have hairs on the lower surface, which is usually lighter in color. There's a broad midrib with dark veins on the underside of the leaf. In the fall, they turn yellow to reddish-purple.

FLOWER: Usually, persimmons are dioecious (they have separate males and females), but some have gorgeous flowers. Flowers bloom from May to June, with white to greenish-yellow flowers. Male blossoms come in clusters of two to three, while females are solitary and bell-shaped, with four recurved petals on each bloom.

FRUIT/SEED/NUT: Between September and December, female trees bear edible fruit that is yellowish to orange. The spherical berries are 1 to 1 1/2 inches long with a waxy bloom and display in yellow, peach, and pale orange colors.

Look-a-likes: There are, in fact, few look-a-likes of persimmons, but make sure you only eat them when they're perfectly ripe.

Caution: Unripe persimmons aren't toxic but unpleasant if they are not fully ripe.

Culinary Uses: Ripe persimmons can be eaten raw, but you do have to spit out the seeds. Use the pulp as a topping or make jams, other sweet treats, or even wine. You can freeze the pulp for later use.

Medicinal Info/Uses: The traditional medicinal use of this plant includes treating sore throats and mouths, indigestion, and thrush.

Fun/Historical Fact: Beer became a staple among enslaved plantation workers in the South, who had limited access to fresh, drinkable water. There is mention of the Southern enslaved people enjoying the brew, commonly combined with such additions as sweet potatoes and apple peels.

The Confederacy found several alternative uses for the persimmon. The strong seeds were made into buttons and roasted to produce a coffee substitute.

Pet Toxicity: Not toxic to your furry friends, but the seeds could cause a blockage in the intestines.

Purple Passionflower

Passiflora incarnata [PASS-IFF-FLOR-uh IN-KAR-NAH-tuh]

The Purple Passionflower is sometimes known as maypop, true passionflower, wild apricot, and wild passion vine. These flowers are more than beautiful; they are brilliantly useful wild edibles. You can use them for culinary and medicinal purposes alike.

Passion flowers grow in full or partial sun in well-drained soil. It grows abundantly in thickets, disturbed areas, pastures, meadows, and rivers.

Identification:

GROWTH/SIZE: The purple passionflower climbs with axillary tendrils or sprawls along the ground. It's an herbaceous vine that can grow up to 25 feet long.

BARK/STEM/ROOT: The green, smooth, coarse-grained bark covers the tree.

LEAF: There are two prominent glands on the leaf stalk; the leaves are three-lobed and dark green above and light green below. In the fall, the leaves change to yellow.

FLOWER: The fragrant flowers bloom from May to July with purple crown fringes, ten white petals and sepals, and pinkish-purple filaments in the middle.

FRUIT/SEED/NUT: Maypops have fleshy, egg-shaped fruits that appear from July to October and mature to a yellowish color with brown seeds.

55

Look-a-likes: Not every passion flower is edible, so ensure you correctly identify the plants.

Caution: If you're considering this for your edible landscape, you shouldn't plant it in your home's defensible space since it's highly flammable.

Culinary Uses: You can create a tincture or tea with the flowers. The fruit is both sour and sweet; you can eat them raw.

Medicinal Uses: The passionflower root made into tea is said to have several potential uses, including diarrhea, menstrual cramps, nerve pain, burns, hemorrhoids, and insomnia. Native Americans treated wounds, cuts, bruises, earaches, and inflammation with poultices made from the root. In addition to eating it, you could drink tea made from it to soothe your nerves.

Fun/Historical Fact: How did the name "Maypop" come about? You don't want to step on the egg-shaped green fruits because they "may pop." P. incarnata gets its name from this phenomenon. Its roots can stay underground for most of the winter, then "pop" up from the ground in May, unharmed by the winter.

Pet Toxicity: Not toxic to your furry friends, so if you are looking for a safe houseplant, Purple Passionflower is the one for you.

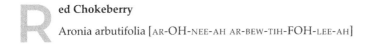

R ed Chokeberry
Aronia arbutifolia [AR-OH-NEE-AH AR-BEW-TIH-FOH-LEE-AH]

Red chokeberries, native to the Eastern United States, are multi-stemmed *deciduous* shrubs that can be enjoyed year-round. Also known as Aronia berries, they are very good for you as they're full of antioxidants. They are a part of the *Rosaceae* (Rose) family and come in two types, Red and Black.

These berries are found on shrubs that prefer full sun. The shrubs grow on sandy soil in woods, swamps, and lakes.

Identification:

GROWTH/SIZE: It grows slowly and is multi-stemmed. Growing 6-12 feet tall and 3-6 feet wide, it typically grows in a vase shape but tends to sucker and form colonies. Fibrous roots and an upright habit characterize the plant.

BARK/STEM/ROOT: The twigs are brownish-red, multiple, and upright. There are red buds encircling the stems. During the winter, the bark is reddish-brown in color, smooth in texture, and exfoliating in nature. A shrub's bark turns grayish-brown as it ages.

LEAF: There are three types of leaves: *oblongs, obovate,* and *ellipticals*. Their size ranges from 1 to 3 1/2 inches long and 1 1/2 inches wide. There's a glossy, smooth surface on the top of the leaf, and the color varies from medium green to dark green. There's a grayish-green pubescence on the underside of the leaf. During October, the leaves turn orange to bright red.

FLOWER: The 5-petaled flowers are white to light pink and have red anthers. They're about one inch in diameter and bloom in May. The nectar they produce attracts butterflies and bees.

FRUIT/SEED/NUT: The fruits ripen from September to November and can last through winter. As the fruit matures, it turns into a glossy red berry. The berries are a quarter to a third of an inch wide and are clustered along the branches. Each pome has one to five seeds.

Look-a-likes: Although chokeberries look like toxic buckthorn berries, the leaves look nothing alike. Buckthorn leaves are usually glossy and a bit more round. Another way to tell them apart is that chokeberry plants do not possess thorns, unlike buckthorn bushes with sharp, long spikes.

Caution: You may want to avoid chokeberries in large quantities if you have a history of urinary stones. Chokeberries contain oxalic acid, a naturally occurring substance in some fruits and vegetables, known to increase the growth of stones.

Culinary Uses: Chokeberries are a great addition to ice cream and fruit salads. They can also be pressed into juice or added to cakes, muffins, tarts, and pies. Dried chokeberries can be eaten alone or added to other recipes. Chokeberry syrup has been used in a variety of recipes.

Medicinal Uses: Studies have shown that regular consumption of chokeberries may offer potential health benefits against cancer, aging and neurological diseases, inflammation, diabetes, and bacterial infections.

Fun/Historical Fact: Native Americans have used all parts of the plant for centuries to fight diseases, increase nutrition, cure meats, and dye materials.

Pet Toxicity: The berries themselves are not toxic, but the seed inside and the plant contain cyanide, which can be deadly to your furry friends.

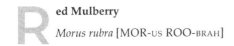

Red Mulberry
Morus rubra [MOR-us ROO-brah]

This bush is native to the Mid-Atlantic region. It's hardy, can grow in virtually any soil, and endure various climate conditions. The fruit, however, is incredibly fragile, which means a couple of things.

- They're never found in grocery stores because they don't travel well.
- It would be best to use them quickly once picked, as they have a short shelf life.

Because Mulberries do so well in multiple climates and soils, you can find mulberries in backyards, gardens, parks, and fields.

Identification:

GROWTH/SIZE: A native, rapidly growing tree that ranges from 25 - 60 feet tall to 35-40 feet wide. The trunk is usually short, making it look like a shrub, while the crown is dense and large.

BARK/STEM/ROOT: The young shoots are usually light green and glabrous. The bark and twigs are brown, reddish-brown, gray, and smooth, with white lenticels scattered throughout.

LEAF: There are heart-shaped, thin, toothed, dark-green leaves 3 to 5 inches long and 2 to 4 inches broad. The leaves can range from unlobed to profoundly lobed and rough-textured to glabrous on the upper surface. The underside of the leaf has fine, soft hair. The leaves on new shoots are more likely to be lobbed, and the leaves on tree crowns are more likely to be unlobed. As fall approaches, the leaves turn yellow.

FLOWER: Flowers bloom from April to May. Unisex greenish flowers appear in early spring in small spikes formed by catkins, with male and female flowers usually growing on separate trees.

FRUIT/SEED/NUT: In May, the tree produces blackberry-like fruits that start red and turn dark purple. Usually, you can find fruit until June if the animals haven't beaten you to it.

Look-a-likes: No known toxic look-a-likes.

Caution: Wear gloves when harvesting them because they will stain your fingers.

Culinary Uses: Mulberries taste similar to blackberries but aren't as tart. You can eat them raw or used as you would other berries, freeze them, make jam, bake them into a pie, or think of something extraordinary to do with them.

Medicinal Uses: Mulberries have many uses as therapeutic aids. The root has been used to treat coughing, wheezing, and edema. The leaves have been used to induce sweating to treat fever, flu, and dysentery. The branches have been used as a muscle relaxer to relieve symptoms of arthritis. And finally, the fruits have been used as a tonic to treat anemia, insomnia, and graying hair.

Fun/Historical Fact: Mulberries look like oddly long blackberries, so if you see a tree growing what looks like blackberries, then you've likely found a mulberry tree, look out for purple stains on the ground where berries have fallen.

During the early explorations of eastern Virginia in 1607, the English mentioned the abundance of mulberry trees and fruit, which the native Powhatan tribes ate.

Heartwood is also used for fence posts because it's durable. Farm implements, cooperage, furniture, interior finishes, and caskets are wood-made.

Pet Toxicity: No known toxicity for your pup, but in large quantities may cause an upset stomach.

American Red Raspberry

Rubus idaeus var. strigosus [ROO-ʙᴜs ᴇʏᴇ-DAY-ᴇᴇ-ᴜs sᴛʀɪɢ-OH-sᴜs]

If you've found a patch of raspberries nearby, you're in for a treat. These soft little berries are sweet, tasty, and easy to harvest. Just make sure that you beat the birds to the punch. It belongs to the **Rosaceae** (rose) family and is known by several names, such as Dewberry, Grayleaf, or Red Raspberry.

You can find wild raspberries along field edges, on old farmland, and the edge of wooded areas. You can also find them in meadows, disturbed areas, or near water or streams.

Identification:

Growth/Size: They are not fast growers but can grow 9 feet tall and just as round.

Bark/Stem/Root: The young stems are green but will change to purple as they mature. As the season progresses, the bark will start to peel. The bark is also covered in glandular hair and sharp thorns.

Leaf: Most leaves have 3-5 leaflets, but some can be undivided, with pleated wrinkles. There's a lighter underside, and it's fuzzy.

Flower: Each flower has five petals, five sepals, five bracts, numerous stamens, and several pistils clustered on a cone-shaped core known as a receptacle that blooms from April through June.

Fruit/Seed/Nut: In botanical terms, the fruits are not berries. Even though they are called berries, they contain many small drupes. The fruits are held together in a hollow cone about 1 inch by 1 inch. They can be found in orange, red, or burgundy, and there is also a black raspberry variety. Remember, raspberries do not ripen after they have been harvested, so make sure they are ripe before picking.

Look-a-likes: There are several look-a-likes to the red raspberry. Most are a part of the same genus - Rubus. Examples are blackberry, dewberry, wineberry, cloudberry, and thimbleberry. Each has a different color flower, but all are edible.

Caution: Watch out for the thorns when harvesting.

Culinary Uses: Raspberries are delicious raw or used as a garnish. You can also freeze them and use them in smoothies or raspberry syrup.

Medicinal Uses: Red raspberry leaf tea is often called "the woman's herb." They can be made into a medicinal tea that is particularly helpful during menstruation. The leaves contain fragrarine, which helps tone and strengthen the pelvic muscles, possibly reducing menstrual cramps.

Fun/Historical Fact: Take a look at the botanical name. In Greek, Rubus means "red," and Idaeus means "belonging to Ida." According to Greek mythology, raspberries were once white until a nymph named Ida pricked her finger while picking the berries for Zeus; her blood stained the berries red. Making the botanical name Rubus idaeus appear much more logical.

Another old myth, this time from Germany, states raspberries have magical properties. Bewitched horses were said to be tamed by tying wild raspberry twigs around their bodies. I agree with the magical properties. Nothing is better than finding a ripe raspberry bush and filling your bucket to overflowing!

Pet Toxicity: Not toxic to your furry friends.

Woodland Strawberry
fragaria virginiana [FRAH-GAR-EE-AH VIR-JIN-EE-AN-UH]

The Woodland Strawberry, also known as wild strawberries, is much smaller than commercial strawberries. If you get a chance, you'll find a deliciously sweet treat that may overshadow the strawberries you're used to seeing in the store. It's a part of the **Rosacea** (rose) family and has no other familiar names.

Wild strawberries grow in patches in fields and dry openings and at the edges of forests where the soil drains well, and there is a good balance of sunlight, shade, and water.

Identification:

GROWTH/SIZE: a ground-hugging native herbaceous perennial that typically grows 4-7 inches tall but can spread indefinitely through runners or **stolons**, which root and expand into new plants as they spread along the ground.

BARK/STEM/ROOT: usually red, and the stems are hairy. New growth starts green and turns red with age.

LEAF: Oval in shape, the leaflet has coarse teeth on the edges except at the bottom. The upper surface of the numerous trifoliate leaves is green, and the lower surface is pale green; an average leaflet measures 3 inches long and 1 1/2 inches wide.

FLOWER: It has white flowers with five petals and numerous ***pistils*** surrounded by yellow ***stamens***. Under the petals are ten small green ***sepals***. They flower in the spring, summer, and fall.

FRUIT/SEED/NUT: Strawberry seeds develop from the pistils in the center of the flower, becoming dark-colored fruits on the plant. The fruits are botanically classified as ***aggregate accessory fruits*** but are commonly called berries.

Look-a-likes: There is only one look-a-like to the wild strawberry, called a Mock strawberry. Though the berries look relatively the same, a few key differences give them away. The wild strawberry has a white to pinkish flower with five petals, grows downward, is juicy and smooth in texture, and has a sweet taste. The Mock strawberry has five-petaled yellow flowers that grow upward; the surface is dry and bumpy and, if eaten, would be tart and unappealing.

Caution: plant allergies are always a chance when harvesting something new. Though no known warnings exist for these little beauties, always use common sense while foraging.

Culinary Uses: Wild strawberries should be eaten, frozen, or processed within hours of Harvest as they can spoil rapidly. Use them as you would commercial strawberries.

Medicinal Uses: Medicinal properties of the whole plant include antiseptic, astringent, and anti-arthritic properties. Nursing mothers have used it to increase milk production and regulate menstrual cycles. The leaves make an astringent tea that is used as a nerve tonic. Dried powdered leaves mixed with oil have been applied as a poultice to treat open sores. It is possible to make tea from roots that have diuretic properties. A few of its many uses are treating diarrhea, irregular menses, gonorrhea, stomach disorders, and lung problems.

Fun/Historical Fact: Store-bought strawberries are hybrids between Fragaria virginiana, indigenous to North America, and Fragaria chiloensis, indigenous to western coastal South America. You get a sweeter, larger fruit by combining the North American wild fruit with the South American one.

Pet Toxicity: Not toxic to your furry friends.

Wineberry

Rubus phoenicolasius [ROO-bus fee-nee-ko-LAY-see-us]

The Wineberry is one of the many wonders of Maryland. While native to Japan, they are so prolific in Maryland that they're considered an invasive shrub which is excellent for foragers as this means there's all the more to enjoy. It's also a part of the **Rosacea** (rose) family, and some of the other common names are Blackberry, Dewberry, Japanese wineberry, and Wine raspberry.

Wineberries are typically found in forests and parks, but you can find them almost everywhere. A moist, well-drained soil is preferred but does well on sandy, loamy, or clay soils.

Identification:

Growth/Size: It grows in extensive thickets; each plant can grow 9 feet tall by 3 feet wide.

Bark/Stem/Root: The canes (branches) have red glandular hairs. If adding this to your edible landscape, it is vital to prune carefully to avoid removing the canes that will produce next year's fruits and flowers. Wineberry only produces fruits on the previous year's branches.

Leaf: The leaves are bright green on the top, alternate, compound, and toothed in three heart-shaped directions. The undersides of the leaves are silvery and highly hairy.

FLOWER: The flower buds are red, hairy, and look like a seed pod. The tiny flowers that emerge are white and star-shaped with pointed-tipped petals. It is in bloom during June and July.

FRUIT/SEED/NUT: The fruit remains enclosed in its calyx until it is about to become ripe. The aggregate drupes measure approximately 3/4 inches in diameter and range from orange to red. August and September are the months when the fruit ripens.

Look-a-likes: Blackberries, Red and black raspberries, and Salmonberries are the only look-a-likes of the wineberry, all of which are edible and have a similar taste.

Caution: Like the other brambles we have reviewed, the wineberry has sharp thorns along the stems, so wearing leather gloves is advised while harvesting.

Culinary Uses: These berries are best eaten as soon as possible and have a short shelf life. You can eat them raw, bake them into pies and desserts, make them into jams or jellies, or preserve them that day by freezing or dehydrating them.

Medicinal Uses: Wineberries have remarkable antioxidant properties that prevent cell damage and promote tissue repair. It is said to inhibit cancer (particularly skin cancer and breast cancer). Because of its natural vitamin C content, it boosts the immune system, reduces inflammation, and helps prevent seasonal allergies.

Fun/Historical Fact: The Māori word for wineberry is makomako or mako. Makomako leaves were boiled and applied topically to treat burns and infected wounds. By squeezing the berries, kids can make a thick, sweet drink. You can dye with wineberries in many ways: the plant has tannins, and its bark is blue-black. They burned wineberry shoots for gunpowder in Europe, turning the wood into charcoal.

Pet Toxicity: Not toxic to your furry friends.

PART FOUR
HERBS AND GREENS

American Pokeweed

Phytolacca americana [FY-TOH-LAK-uh A-MER-IH-KAY-NAH]

American Pokeweed is a somewhat contentious plant among gardeners and foragers. It's an invasive weed, like many wild edibles, but it can be toxic if you aren't careful. However, pokeweed can become a fantastic seasonal treat if you know what you're doing. It's part of the *Phytolaccaceae* (pokeweed) family and has several common names, such as Garnet, Pigeon Berry, Pokeberry, and Scoke.

© Skyler Principe CC by 4.0

Forest edges, fence rows, power lines, old fields, openings in forests, and pastures are all excellent places to find them. There are times when it's a weed in the garden or yard.

Identification:

GROWTH/SIZE: Mature pokeweed is easy to locate but is a poisonous, herbaceous perennial plant. It grows 4-10 feet high, is aggressive, self-seeding, and can become weedy.

BARK/STEM/ROOT: An underground taproot can become significant over a few years and produce one or more stems. Stems are usually pinkish-red, smooth, partly hollow, not very strong, and up to 2 inches across.

LEAF: Green on top and lighter below; the leaves are alternate and thin. Leaf size is

69

usually 7 to 14 inches long by 4 to 7 inches wide, and both ends are tapered. When crushed or bruised, some leaves and stems smell unpleasant.

FLOWER: Pinkish racemes are on short stems, with each flower displayed in a linear cluster. In most cases, the flowers are white to greenish but can also be pinkish or purple. Each flower has five sepals, no petals, and about ten stamens.

FRUIT/SEED/NUT: Between June and November, they're in bloom. Pokeweed has drooping clusters of green fruit that turn glossy purple-black when matured. The seeds are about 1/4 inch across and have 6 to 12 each. Small mammals and birds usually flock to them.

Look-a-likes: Pokeweed shoots look like dogbane shoots, which are toxic. However, dogbane leaves grow in opposite pairs, and when broken, dogbane produces a milky white sap. Mature pokeweed is toxic, so you should only harvest it when young and the stem is pliable.

Caution: Symptoms include diarrhea and vomiting. The plant contains chemicals that can damage chromosomes and cause cell division.

Culinary Uses: Pokeweed needs to be cooked before eating. You should boil it for 5-10 minutes, then drain the water. Boil it a second time before frying.

Medicinal Uses: Berries were used as a poultice for sore breasts and roots as a remedy for rheumatism, neuralgia, and bruises; wash was used for sprains, swellings, and leaf preparations were used as expectorants. Juice is emetic and cathartic, used as a poultice to treat bleeding, acne, pimples, and blackheads.

Fun/Historical Fact: Allen Canning Co. in Arkansas jumped on the bandwagon but sadly produced their last batch of Poke Sallet in the spring of 2000. Because it was the first spring green, it provided a welcome change to the winter's menu.

Pet Toxicity: All parts of this plant are poisonous to pets. Symptoms include vomiting, spasms, and severe convulsions, resulting in death if not seen by a vet.

B

lack Cohosh

actaea racemosa [AK-TAY-AH RAY-SEE-MO-SAH]

As far back as 2000 years ago, the Native Americans have been using the roots and tubers of this plant to make herbal tea. Black Cohosh is a member of the *Ranunculaceae* (buttercup) family. It's known by several other names, black snakeroot, bugbane, bugwort, rattleroot, and rattleweed, and it is a native North American plant.

It's in shady areas, typically near tall hardwood trees.

Identification:

GROWTH/SIZE: With a medium growth rate, it can grow as large as 7 feet tall and 4 feet wide.

BARK/STEM/ROOT: It's got a wiry black-purple stem with a mildly unpleasant, medicinal smell at close range.

LEAF: The **deciduous, basal** leaves form repeated sets of **tripinnately compound** leaflets three feet long and wide. There are usually three lobes on the terminal leaflet. They're obovate to ovate-lanceolate in outline, 2-5 lobed, and toothed or incised on the margins.

FLOWER: On long stems that reach 30 to 98 inches tall, the flowers form *racemes* up to 20 inches long in late spring and early summer. The flowers are a tight cluster of 55–110 white *stamens* surrounded by a white stigma, with no petals or *sepals*. Its sweet, stinky smell attracts flies, gnats, and beetles.

Look-a-likes: Make sure that the roots are thoroughly washed. Use small doses of black cohosh and, when Harvest, take care to preserve the plant.

Caution: You might get nausea, dizziness, visual effects, a low heart rate, and sweat when you take black cohosh in high doses. Despite its common name, blue cohosh (Caulophyllum thalictroides) belongs to another family, *Berberidaceae*, which is not closely related to black cohosh, and together they may be hazardous.

Culinary Uses: Wash the roots thoroughly. You can then use them to make a medicinal tea or tincture.

Medicinal Uses: 83 reports of liver damage associated with black cohosh, including hepatitis, liver failure, and elevated liver enzymes. However, a cause-and-effect relationship remains unclear. Millions of women have taken black cohosh without getting sick, and a meta-analysis of clinical trials found no damage to liver function.

Pet Toxicity: Though it is not labeled as toxic on the ASPCA website, ingestion of large amounts can cause upset stomach, vomiting, and diarrhea in some cases.

loodroot

Sanguinaria canadensis [SAN-GWIN-AR-ee-uh ka-na-DEN-sis]

Bloodroot belongs to the **Papaveraceae** (poppy) family. It goes by several names, such as Coon root, Indian plant, snakebite, sweet slumber, paucon, red root, and tetterwort. It isn't usually ingested; it's transformed into a tincture for external uses. It has been known to have several benefits, making it a good option for foragers.

Bloodroot is mainly found in moist to dry woods and thickets, usually along shorelines and close to streams on slopes and floodplains. They're less common in clearings, meadows, dunes, and disturbed areas.

Identification:

GROWTH/SIZE: The plant grows 6-10 inches tall in the wild and spreads to form large colonies on the forest floor.

BARK/STEM/ROOT: The stem grows straight from the rhizome and resembles a flower stalk.

LEAF: The plant has one big basal leaf, 10 inches wide, and five to nine lobed leaves with blunt teeth that last until midsummer.

FLOWER: Flowers bloom between March and May, depending on the region. Flowers emerge from the ground with leaves clasping them. Once bloomed, the flower consists of eight to twelve delicate white petals, many yellow stamens, and two sepals below the petals that fall off. Sunlight opens the flowers, and darkness closes them.

Fruit/Seed/Nut: The fruits are green pods with brown seeds ready in April-May. The seeds develop in green pods that ripen before the foliage turns dormant. When ripe, seeds are round, black to orange-red, with white elaiosomes that ants eat.

Look-a-likes: Bloodroot is a medicinal plant and shouldn't be ingested. When using it on your skin, test it on a small area to ensure that you don't have a bad reaction, as some people experience skin irritation.

Caution: In the bloodroot, the juice is red and poisonous. It can cause nausea, vomiting, faintness, dizziness, dilated pupils, fainting, diarrhea, and heart failure. Products from sanguinaria extracts, such as black salve, are escharotic and can cause permanent disfiguring scarring. Although preliminary studies have suggested that sanguinaria may have potential applications in cancer therapy, clinical studies are lacking, and its use is not recommended.

Culinary Uses: You can combine the sap with water and put it on your skin to repel mosquitos. Perfect when you're out foraging, and bugs won't leave you alone.

Medicinal Uses: Mainly a folk remedy for skin issues, Native Americans have long used bloodroot to treat various ailments, including sore throats, congestion, respiratory conditions, hemorrhoids, irregular menstruation, and wound infections. It has also been used to induce abortions. Modern herbalists offer a tincture to help remove growths, warts, and cancerous cells.

Other uses include a stain for furniture and an excellent natural mosquito repellent.

Fun/Historical Fact: Bloodroot seeds are spread by ants through a process known as *myrmecochory*.

Pet Toxicity: The entire plant is toxic to dogs, be sure to contact your vet immediately if you see your pet eating this.

B lue Violet
Viola sororia [vy-OH-la so-ROR-ee-uh]

The Romans would wear headdresses covered in violets when drinking because they thought they would give them the feeling of drunkenness without the aftermath. As you could have guessed, they are a part of the **Violaceae** (violet) family. These plants are called Dooryard Violet, Hooded Blue, and Meadow Violet. They are commonly used both for culinary and medicinal purposes.

You can find these nifty little plants at the beginning of spring as they're among the first plants to bloom. They grow in woods, thickets, and along stream beds, especially in shadier areas.

Identification:

Growth/Size: A fast-growing **herbaceous perennial** wildflower usually grows in a clump. It can grow as large as 10 inches tall and just as wide.

Bark/Stem/Root: stemless

Leaf: The leaf blades are yellowish-green, **simple, cordate,** acute, serrate to crenate, pubescent underneath, and subpeltate, reaching 4 inches wide; the stipule leaf blades are linear-lanceolate. Depending on the growing conditions, the color of the leaves may vary.

FLOWER: Despite their purple hue, the purple flowers have white throats and three hairy petals at the bottom. The erect stem of the flower droops slightly, and the flowers bend toward the ground.

FRUIT/SEED/NUT: The fruits are available in a 3-chambered capsule from April and June.

Look-a-likes: `Lesser Celandine`, a toxic plant with leaves similar to wild violets, has yellow flowers.

Caution: Only harvest blue or purple flowers. Yellow violets aren't edible. There's a chance that violet roots can cause nausea and vomiting, so don't eat them.

Culinary Uses: You can eat raw leaves or blossoms and use them in salads. The flowers can also make syrups, jelly and jams, and violet sugar. The leaves can be cooked or made into violet tea. Wild violets are high in vitamin C and very good for you.

Medicinal Uses: Traditionally, plant infusions have been used to combat dysentery, coughs, and colds. Headaches can be treated with a poultice made from leaves. Boils have been treated with a dressing of crushed roots.

Fun/Historical Fact: Persephone, daughter of Zeus and Hera, picked violets when she was sent to the Underworld to marry Hades, making them more of a funeral flower during the Antiquity period.

Pet Toxicity: non-toxic for your pup.

Burdock Root
Arctium lappa [ARK-tee-um LAP-uh]

The Burdock root is commonly used for medicinal purposes but is also edible. It is a part of the **Asteraceae** (daisy) family and is known by several other names. Bardane, Beggar's Buttons, Gobo, Lappa, Snake's Rhubarb, and Thorny Burr are just a few. In its first year, burdock grows as a vegetative plant (roots, shoots, leaves). On the other hand, burdock flower stalks are best collected in the spring or early summer of the second year.

Burdock grows in disturbed areas, empty lots, parks, roadsides, fields, and pastures.

Identification:

GROWTH/SIZE: It can grow ten feet tall and four feet wide.

LEAF: These plants have broad, heart-shaped leaves with woolly hairs underneath. The leaves are most prominent at the base of the plant, and they get smaller as they go up. Leaves with solid stalks have grooves on the upper surface. It has simple, alternating leaves. They can be lobed or unlobed, but they don't have leaflets. Each node on the stem has only one leaf.

FLOWER: The purple globular flowerheads are arranged in flat-headed cymes about

1-1.5 inches in diameter. Flowers have needle-thin bracts and many disk florets that end in a sharp tip with a hook.

Fruit/Seed/Nut: As the flowers die, the bracts turn brown, forming a sharp burr covered in loops. Seeds can be dispersed more easily with this design since it clings to animal fur, bird feathers, or clothing. You may need help getting rid of burs.

Caution: Like other weeds, harvest from an area that hasn't been sprayed with herbicides.

Culinary Uses: You can eat every part of the plant, and it resembles artichokes in taste. Watch for the flower stalk to form in the middle. You'll want to harvest it before the flowers bloom; usually, it'll be 2-3 feet tall by then. Cut it close to the ground and remove the leaves; there will be anywhere from 1/2 inch to 1 1/2 inch thick stems. It will be too tough to eat if it's hollow in the middle. Trim up the stalk until you get to a solid core. There's a big difference between the bitter, fibrous exterior and the tender, pale interior. Using a paring knife, remove the outer skin. You can cook burdock flower stalks the same way you cook artichokes. Pasta, casseroles, and salads are all delicious ways to use them. To get a feel for how it tastes, use a simple preparation. Once the stalks are peeled, chop them into chunks, boil until easily pierced, and serve with butter, salt, and pepper.

Medicinal Uses: Chinese and Western herbal medicine utilize burdock as a detoxifying herb. Aside from the dried roots of a one-year-old plant, the leaves and fruits can also be consumed. It treats conditions like throat infections, boils, rashes, and other skin problems.

Fun/Historical Fact: In 1941, George de Mestral, a Swiss engineer, was on a hunting trip with his dog. When he got home, he realized he was covered in burs, and so was the dog. He looked at the burs under a microscope and saw thousands of tiny hooks. He figured out how to use the hooks and loop them in fabrics. In 1955, he filed for his patent on what we all know and use today, Velcro.

Pet Toxicity: It is perfectly safe for dogs. It can be given regularly to aid in detoxification or to help the liver, bladder, and kidneys remain healthy. See the recipe section for how to create the decoction.

C hickweed

Stellaria media [STELL-AR-ee-uh MEED-ee-uh]

Chickweed grows everywhere, which is excellent news for foragers because it's almost as tasty as it is nutritious. It's part of the *Caryophyllaceae* (carnation) family and has multiple names, such as starweed, Birdweed, Chickenwort, Starweed, Starwort, Winterweed, and mouse ear.

Chickweed grows almost everywhere, including backyards, parks, grasslands, fields, and wastelands.

Identification:

GROWTH/SIZE: It grows in large patches, forming mats that can grow to 1-2 feet tall and round.

BARK/STEM/ROOT: The succulent stems are green or burgundy and often have white hairs.

LEAF: The leaves are *oval-ovate*, to broadly *elliptic* along their margins, hairless on top, and occasionally hairy on the bottom. The stems at the bottom of the plant have short, hairy *petioles*, while the leaves near the tip are *sessile*. They are more prominent at the ends of the stems, spanning up to ¾ inch in length and ½ inch across.

79

FLOWER: There are white, small flowers with distinctly lobed petals. In most cases, there are three stamens and three styles. The flowers don't take long to form capsules; a plant can have both flowers and capsules.

FRUIT/SEED/NUT: Seed capsules replace each flower; they're light brown, with six small teeth along their upper rim and several seeds. Mature seeds are reddish brown, slightly flattened, and orbicular-reniform; they have minute bumps on their surface.

Look-a-likes: One toxic look-alike is the scarlet pimpernel. You can tell the difference by looking for the line of fine hairs along the stem, as the scarlet pimpernel doesn't have it. The flowers are also reddish-orange, and the plant itself has milky sap.

Caution: Nausea, upset stomach, diarrhea, and vomiting can result from too much chickweed.

Culinary Uses: You can eat chickweed raw in salads or use it to make pestos or green smoothies. Chickweed will keep in the fridge for a few days if you wrap it in a damp paper towel and put it in a plastic bag. It also freezes reasonably well if you blend it up first.

Medicinal Uses: Soothing, cooling, hydrating, and healing, chickweed has it all. For skin inflammation, wounds, boils, rashes, acne, and drawing out infections. It's applied topically as a plant poultice or infused in olive oil. Our ability to absorb nutrients improves when we eat chickweed. Combining this with the high fiber and mineral content makes chickweed a highly effective digestive support aid.

Fun/Historical Fact: Chickweed makes excellent food for poultry as well.

Pet Toxicity: Chickweed is not toxic for dogs; quite the opposite. There are several uses for chickweed when it comes to your best friend.

- **Hotspots and Skin irritation:** make a poultice using chickweed to soothe burns, hotspots, and skin irritations.
- **Tinctures:** used as an astringent to help clean and heal minor skin wounds by applying juice fresh from the stem.
- **Tea:** because it's tasty and easy for pups to digest, it can be used to soothe the occasional upset stomach.

C hicory
Cichorium intybus [sik-KOR-ee-um IN-tye-bus]

Chicory is incredibly common, and once you know what to look for, you'll probably find it everywhere. It belongs to the *Asteraceae* (daisy) family. It is known by several names, such as blue daisy, blue dandelion, blue sailors, blueweed, coffee weed, cornflower, horseweed, and wild endive.

Chicory grows readily in disturbed areas, like wastelands, meadows, fields, and roadsides.

Identification:

Growth/Size: This biennial plant grows from two to four feet tall and one foot wide.

Bark/Stem/Root: It has erect green or reddish-brown stems with a fleshy taproot that exudes a milky sap when cut.

Leaf: Generally, *alternate* leaves are up to eight inches long and two inches wide, becoming smaller as they ascend the stem. These leaves are *lance-shaped* and resemble dandelion leaves at the base. The leaves gradually narrow where they are *sessile* or clasp the stem. Depending on where the leaves are on the branch, they have lobed edges, dentate edges, or they lose their *petioles* and hold the stem. In the lower leaf surface, the central vein usually has many hairs.

81

FLOWER: With numerous bright blue rays and blunt-toothed edges, these flowers have *ligulate flower heads* up to 1.5 inches long. These flowers have no stalks and grow along stems, opening up in the morning and closing up by noon unless it's cloudy, appearing from mid-summer until the first frost.

FRUIT/SEED/NUT: Has *achene* with a brown oval shape, five ribs, and blunt ends. On the broader end, there are bristles across the top.

Look-a-likes: Chicory plants are distinctive with their flowers and have no toxic relatives. Only dandelions and daisies are easier to identify among wildflowers for a beginner forager.

Caution: Chicory might have been sprayed with herbicides as it's considered a weed. Avoid harvesting chicory that's too close to busy roads.

Culinary Uses: The leaves and flowers are bitter and can be used in salads. Use sparingly and, if need be, blanch the leaves to take away some of the bitterness. In addition, chicory roots can also be roasted, ground, or blended with coffee to make a less expensive and caffeine-free beverage.

Medicinal Uses: In the laboratory, root extracts have also been shown to be antibacterial, anti-inflammatory, and mildly sedative. In addition, they slow down and weaken the pulse, as well as lower blood sugar levels. Extracts from leaves have similar effects, though they are weaker. To treat swellings, bruised leaves were used as a poultice. A root extract can treat fevers and jaundice, as well as as a diuretic and laxative.

Fun/Historical Fact: You can spot chicory by looking for distinctive blueish-purple flowers. Initially brought to the United States by the colonists as a medicinal herb, chicory was cultivated by Thomas Jefferson and others as a forage crop. As it does not dry well, horses, cattle, sheep, poultry, and rabbits were usually fed it fresh.

Pet Toxicity: Chicory is pet-safe and can benefit your pet's health.

D andelion
Daraxacum officinale [TA-RAKS-uh-kum oh-fiss-ih-NAH-lee]

Dandelions are one of the most common edibles and are found all over the world. They're easy to spot, which makes them a fantastic foraging option for beginners. They belong to the *Asteraceae* (daisy) family and have only one different name: Lion's tooth.

Dandelions prefer shady, cooler areas, but you'll also find them in direct sunlight. To the distaste of many homeowners, they grow on lawns. Potential habitats include parks, pastures, orchards, hayfields, meadows, and disturbed areas such as roadsides and wastelands.

Identification:

GROWTH/SIZE: You can quickly identify Dandelions by their distinctive yellow blooms. It is a fast-spreading broadleaf perennial weed that spreads by seed. The plant grows 2-6 inches tall and can get as wide as 2 feet.

BARK/STEM/ROOT: Leafless and unbranched hollow stems form deep taproots, and milky latex sap flows throughout the plant.

LEAF: A ***basal rosette*** is formed in an ***oblanceolate*** shape. Deeply toothed, backward-pointing teeth or lobes are present on rosette leaves at the base.

FLOWER: A bright yellow ray flower with toothed tips appears throughout the year on second-year plants. In the evening, they close their petals, which are single heads on their stems.

FRUIT/SEED/NUT: Seed heads are fluffy, round, downy, and dispersed by the wind.

Look-a-likes: Cat's Ear (*Hypochaeris radicata*) is the most likely to be mistaken for dandelion, as the flower heads look very similar. Cat's Ear does not have hollow stems, and their stems are branching. They also have hairy leaves with deep notches.

Sow Thistle (*Sonchus spp.*) also does not have hollow stems, and the leaves grow up the entire stalk with multiple flowers growing from each branch. In the thistle family, the mature plant also has prickly spines.

Caution: None plant-related, but be sure to check if they have been sprayed with a weed killer before eating.

Culinary Uses: The entire dandelion plant is edible, but you must prepare the greens and the root differently. The greens can be eaten raw or added to salads, they have an earthy and bitter taste, and it's best to use young leaves. The leaves can also be sautéed in olive oil and garlic and seasoned. Flowers can be used to make dandelion wine, syrups, or even battered and fried like zucchini blossoms. Chopping and roasting the roots can be used to create tea.

Medicinal Uses: The dandelion is a commonly used herbal remedy. It is especially effective and valuable as a diuretic because it contains high levels of potassium salts and can replace the potassium lost from the body when used. The plant is used internally to treat gall bladder and urinary disorders, gallstones, jaundice, cirrhosis, dyspepsia with constipation, edema associated with high blood pressure and heart weakness, chronic joint and skin complaints, gout, eczema, and acne. The latex contained in the plant sap can be used to remove corn, warts, and verrucae.

Fun/Historical Fact: The yellow flowers can be dried and ground into a yellow-pigmented powder and used as a dye.

Pet Toxicity: Dandelion, though not toxic, can cause constipation and gas in some dogs. The dandelion will boost its immune system and help improve digestion. It also aids in building strong bones and teeth.

G arlic Mustard

Alliaria petiolata [AL-EE-AR-EE-UH PET-EE-OH-LAH-TUH]

Garlic mustard is an invasive, destructive weed with a bad habit of drowning out native biodiversity and creating monocultures. The good news is that it's delicious and nutritious, which means that foragers can help themselves and their local forests by harvesting it. It is a part of the **Brassicaceae** family. It goes by several other common names, such as Garlicwort, Hedge Garlic, Jack-in-the-Bush, Mustard Root, Poor Man's Mustard, and Sauce-Alone.

It's common in shady woodland areas and forest edges, but you can also find it in fields, roadsides, and fences.

Identification:

GROWTH/SIZE: Early in the season, and especially in the first year of growth, garlic mustard grows as a herb on the forest floor. It's an herbaceous, biennial, flowering plant that spreads quickly.

BARK/STEM/ROOT: There is occasional hair on the stems of 2nd-year plants. Otherwise, they are glabrous like the blades of leaves.

LEAF: The plant's first year of growth produces clumps of round to heart-shaped leaves roughly two inches long and wide with coarsely toothed edges. The 2nd year plant's alternate leaves are similar to the first year's, except they are more elon-

85

gated, spanning up to three inches long by two inches wide. The leaves smell like garlic when crushed.

FLOWER: No flowers produced during the first year make identifying more tricky. However, during the second year of growth, the upper stems terminate in four-petalled white flowers resembling cross-shaped buttons. The top of the raceme is filled with clusters of these flowers while they're blooming. The raceme, however, becomes more elongated and separated as the flowers mature and develop seedpods.

FRUIT/SEED/NUT: The fruit consists of an elongated, four-sided pod 1 1/2 to 2 inches long. Initially green, it turns gray-brown as it matures. Two rows of shiny black seeds are inside and released when the pod splits open in midsummer. This plant often forms colonies by reseeding itself. It produces hundreds of seeds that can scatter as many as several feet away from the parent plant.

Look-a-likes: Ground ivy has similar leaves but is also edible. If you aren't sure, crush the leaves and smell them. Garlic mustard will smell of garlic.

Caution: As this is an invasive plant, beware when harvesting that it has not been sprayed with chemicals.

Culinary Uses: You can enjoy garlic mustard raw or cook it to neutralize the slight bitterness. Use it to substitute greens and add a fantastic garlicky kick to your meals.

Medicinal Uses: There has been little use of garlic mustard in herbal medicine. Previously, the leaves were taken internally to treat bronchitis, asthma, scurvy, and eczema and promote sweating. The roots are chopped up small and then heated in oil to make an ointment to rub on the chest to relieve bronchitis. The poultices are effective externally applied to ulcers, stings, bites, etc.

Fun/Historical Fact: Originally, garlic mustard was used as a vegetable due to its high vitamin A and C content.

Pet Toxicity: The short answer is yes. In large doses, garlic mustard can be toxic to your pets. It contains glucosinolates and cyanide. Cooking the greens helps to neutralize the toxicity.

American Ginseng

Panax quinquefolius [PAN-aks kwin-kway-FOH-lee-us]

Ginseng is hugely popular in Asia for its medicinal properties and flavor. The good news is that you can also find American ginseng in the wild. Foraging ginseng is far cheaper than purchasing it in the store. It's a part of the ***Araliaceae*** family and is native to North America's Northeastern and Appalachian regions. It is also known as Ground Nut.

It thrives in shaded forests, in areas blessed with moist, well-drained soils, boasting a pH level of around 5.5. Watch for it near babbling streams. Ginseng often chooses to grow on slopes that face north or east, where the sun's rays are gentler. These sheltered inclines create the perfect haven, maintaining the ideal balance of temperature and humidity. As you tread softly, be prepared to uncover this hidden gem beneath a delicate layer of fallen leaves, revealing its precious presence.

Identification:

Growth/Size: The plant reaches between 6 to 18 inches tall

Bark/Stem/Root: The root looks like a small, forking parsnip. They have smooth stems that are reddish-green.

Leaf: The middle leaflet is the largest; the side leaflets become smaller as they go outward. This plant has three, sometimes five, leaflets on its compound leaves, which are medium green. Leaf stalks range in length from 1.4 to 1.25 inches. The shapes range from oblong to lance-like to elliptic, and a whorl of leaflets surrounds the stem, about halfway between the base and flower cluster. Each leaflet has a finely-toothed edge.

FLOWER: A single 1-inch round cluster of flowers appears at the top of the plant. It has five white petals and five white stamens, measuring about an eighth inch across. The flowers turn pale pink with age. It blooms from mid-May through very early June. On years that spring comes early, you may find it in bloom in early May.

FRUIT/SEED/NUT: The flowers are followed by yellow, berry-like fruit later in the summer.

Look-a-likes: Compared with American ginseng (*P. quinquefolius*), it appears minia-ture. The three almost sessile leaflets of Dwarf ginseng can be distinguished from American ginseng's five stalked leaflets.

Caution: Ensure you follow restrictions when Harvesting wild American ginseng. You can only harvest ginseng during certain months; the plant should have at least three compound leaves and be at least five years old.

Culinary Uses: Clean the ginseng root, then let it dry naturally. Once it's dried out a bit, use it as a spice.

Medicinal Uses: There are several health benefits to a regular dose of Ginseng. Increased energy, clearer thinking and cognitive function, anti-inflammatory, and lower blood sugar. However, safe to consume; there have been reports of headaches, insomnia, diarrhea, and rapid heart rate.

Fun/Historical Fact: Cherokee tribes used this herb to treat chest pain, headaches, hives, colic, gout, rheumatism, and liver ailments. The Iroquois used it to treat chest pains and as a medicine for sports.

Pet Toxicity: Ginseng is safe for your pet. It is commonly prescribed by vets to help with the following disorders: Addison's disease, congestive heart failure, diabetes mellitus, chronic low-grade hepatitis, and possibly cognitive dysfunction.

G oldenseal

Hydrastis canadensis [HY-DRASS-TISS KAN-AH-DEN-SIS]

Goldenseal is a slow-growing, native herb often harvested for its roots and used for its medicinal properties versus food. It is a part of the ***Ranunculaceae*** (buttercup) family. It's also called orange root or yellow puccoon.

It grows in mature hardwood forests. You'll generally find it in shady areas near stream banks and slopes.

Identification:

GROWTH/SIZE: It is a perennial herb and typically grows 10-15 inches tall.

BARK/STEM/ROOT: A purplish and hairy stem is found above ground, while a yellow rhizome can be found below ground. Approximately 6–19 inches tall, they are fuzzy, upright, and unbranched.

LEAF: There are two palmately lobed leaves on a single stem of fertile plants. During spring, flowering plants produce a single terminal flower without petals, three sepals, and twelve or more white pistils.

FLOWER: Has two leaves and a single, apetalous, yellowish-green to greenish-white flower with prominent white stamens. The spring season is when flowers bloom.

Fruit/Seed/Nut: The fertilized flowers turn into berries with two or three seeds, which are red and raspberry-like.

Look-a-likes: Some sources suggest that Japanese Barberry, an invasive plant in America, offers many of the same health benefits.

Caution: Goldenseal is susceptible to over-harvesting by foragers. For this reason, the plant is considered at risk. Forage sparingly and give the plant time to recover. There is a low possibility of toxicity if eaten by some people. It produces nausea, vomiting, diarrhea, nervousness, and depression.

Culinary Uses: Clean and dry the roots. You can then use them to make tea, blitzed into a powder.

Medicinal Uses: It contains *berberine*, a compound known to help with digestive issues. Small-scale commercial cultivation has been carried out in the mountains due to the rootstock's use in digestion aids, insect repellents, and as a yellow dye.

Fun/Historical Fact: The maturity of a plant takes between four and five years. A plant in the first stage can remain in this state for one or more years after the seed erupts and cotyledons emerge. After the first vegetative stage, the second occurs in years two and three, sometimes even longer. A single leaf and no well-developed stem are the distinguishing characteristics. The third stage is reproductive, which is characterized by flowering and fruiting. It takes between four and five years for this last stage to develop.

It has been harvested for centuries for its medicinal properties. The Cherokee Indians used the root as a cancer treatment, an antiseptic, an overall health tonic, and to treat snakebite. The Iroquois tribe used it to treat whooping cough, diarrhea, liver trouble, fever, pneumonia, and several digestive disorders. They also mixed the ground roots with bear grease as an insect repellent and boiled them to make a yellow dye.

Pet Toxicity: Considered a "wonder herb" by holistic vets, goldenseal is entirely safe for your pet and can be given dried, powdered, in a tea, or as a tincture.

Japanese Knotweed

Reynoutria japonica [RAY-NU-TREE-AH JUH-PON-IH-KUH]

Japanese Knotweed is an infamously invasive weed that's very hard to subdue or destroy. It's a part of the *Polygonaceae* (buckwheat) family. Other common names are Asiatic Knotweed, Donkey Rhubarb, Fleeceflower, Huzhang, Japanese Bamboo, and Mexican Bamboo. The good news is that you can eat it and do your bit to fight off every gardener's menace.

Japanese knotweed can grow anywhere, especially in a wasteland, disturbed areas, near water, and by roadsides.

Identification:

GROWTH/SIZE: It can grow up to 13 feet tall and 20 feet wide.

BARK/STEM/ROOT: There are large, hollow, slightly ridged, jointed, and mottled stems that range in color from green to reddish-brown. They resemble bamboo and appear after the plant has died back. Near the ground, older stems become woody.

LEAF: Broadly oval to triangular, sharply pointed, alternate leaves with truncated bases and entire margins, 3 to 7 inches long and 2-4 inches wide. A dark green top and a light green bottom with reddish veins distinguish the leaves. There is an ochrea, a sheathing-like structure, where they meet the stem. Growth is red when it is new.

FLOWER: Later summer to fall, the plants have small creamy-white flowers with five tepals in erect panicles 3-6 inches long. The male and female flowers grow on different plants, with the male flowers being more upright and the female flowers drooping.

FRUIT/SEED/NUT: Small, shiny, dark brown to black triangular seeds are in each winged triangular achene.

Look-a-likes: Several plants have been mistakenly identified as knotweeds, including dogwoods, lilacs, ornamental bistorts such as red bistort (Persicaria amplexicaulis), lesser knotweeds, Himalayan balsams, broad-leaved docks (Rumex obtusifolius), bindweeds, bamboo, Himalayan honeysuckle (Leycesteria formosa), and Russian vines.

Caution: As Japanese knotweed is so invasive, specimens may have been sprayed with herbicides or other chemicals. Make sure it's chemical-free. Don't trample on it, as you may spread the weed further.

Culinary Uses: You can substitute asparagus for young spring shoots by cooking them. It has an acidic taste and can also be a rhubarb substitute in pies, fruit soups, jams, etc. Older stems and shoot tips have a mild rhubarb flavor when cooked. It is possible to use the seeds raw or cooked. You can also grind the seeds into a powder and use them as a flavoring and thickener in soups or when you bake bread and cakes.

Medicinal Uses: In Japan, the common name is Itadori, meaning "pain puller" or "removes pain." Because of the high level of resveratrol and its potential to treat neurodegenerative diseases, extensive research has been conducted on the plant. Several studies have shown that these compounds have anti-inflammatory, antimicrobial, antioxidant, and neuroprotective properties.

Fun/Historical Fact: Japanese knotweed is a species of herbaceous perennial plant whose flowers are valued by northeastern beekeepers as a source of nectar for honeybees because it flowers when nothing else is. Japanese knotweed yields honey tasting like the mild-flavored version of buckwheat honey.

Pet Toxicity: Completely safe for your furry friend.

Jerusalem Artichoke

Helianthus tuberosus [HEEL-EE-AN-THUS TOO-BER-OH-SUS]

Jerusalem Artichokes are not, in fact, artichokes from Jerusalem. They are a delicious part of the ***Asteraceae*** (sunflower or daisy) family. They produce enormous amounts of tubers that keep coming back year after year. Common names include Earth Apple, Sunchoke, and Sunroot.

They can grow almost anywhere with plenty of sunlight and water.

Identification:

GROWTH/SIZE: The plant grows 6 - 10 feet tall and 3 - 5 feet wide.

BARK/STEM/ROOT: The top stems rise between 6 and 10 feet and are rough-hairy.

LEAF: The leaves are opposite, hairy, and 2 to 4 inches wide, growing smaller as they go up the stem. Leaves on the lower part of the plant are usually opposite, while leaves on the upper part are generally alternate. Leaves on winged petioles are rough and ovate with serrate-dentate edges.

FLOWER: They have yellow sunflower heads with 2 to 4 inches of showy, petal-like rays surrounding a yellow center disk with tiny dark yellow disk florets. In August and September, the flowers bloom and attract butterflies. The seed heads attract songbirds.

93

Fruit/Seed/Nut: The seed heads ripen in November. The knobby tubers are harvested in the fall, around two weeks after the flowers fade, usually from October to December.

Look-a-likes: A Jerusalem artichoke is sometimes confused with a Globe artichoke (Cynara scolymus); however, the rounded flowers of that plant are edible.

Caution: If you harvest too soon, the tubers will be harder to digest. Make sure that the soil is uncontaminated.

Culinary Uses: The tubers will need washing, and it might be easier to peel them. You can eat raw tubers or pickle them, but many people like to roast them. They can be eaten as roasted root vegetables or a delicious soup. They can be prepared as you would a potato. However, they tend to get soft and mushy when boiled, so steaming or baking is probably the best action. They have a similar consistency to other tubers and, in their raw form, have a similar texture but a sweeter, nuttier flavor. Slice the raw tuber thinly and add a little extra crunch to a salad.

Medicinal Uses: You can use it for digestive health, immune health, and diabetes. It is an excellent prebiotic and nutritious plant-based potassium, iron, and protein source.

Fun/Historical Fact: The end of the 19th century saw most of the Jerusalem artichoke crop in Baden-Württemberg, Germany, used to produce a spirit called "Topinambur-Branntwein," meaning Jerusalem artichoke brandy in German. Jerusalem artichoke brandy has a slight nutty-sweet flavor but smells fruity.

Pet Toxicity: They are perfectly safe for your pets. They are root vegetables which means they are high in fiber and will aid in digestion in your pup.

M allow

Malva neglecta [MAL-ᴠᴜʜ ɴᴇ-GLEK-ᴛᴜʜ]

Mallow is highly nutritious. For centuries, it has been used as food and for medicinal purposes. It belongs to the *Malvaceae* (mallow) family. Its other common names are Buttonweed, Creeping Charlie, Cheeseweed, high mallow, wood mallow, and dwarf mallow.

It grows on grassland, by roadsides, in a wasteland, with scrubs, cultivated gardens, and parks.

Identification:an *annual* or *biennial* invasive weed.

Gʀᴏᴡᴛʜ/Sɪᴢᴇ: The plant grows between 1-4 feet tall.

Bᴀʀᴋ/Sᴛᴇᴍ/Rᴏᴏᴛ: It has a coarse, hairy stem that shoots off single ivy-like leaves.

Lᴇᴀғ: On the stem, the leaves are roundish, with numerous lobes, each 1 - 1 1/2 inches long, 1- 2 inches wide, and 2 to 4 inches in diameter. There are prominent veins on the leaf's underside and hairs radiating from a central point.

Fʟᴏᴡᴇʀ: The flowers are reddish-purple, bright pinkish-purple with dark stripes, or bright mauve-purple with dark stripes. There are 2 to 4 axillary clusters along the main stem, with flowers at the base opening first. The flowers are in bloom from early Spring to early fall.

Fruit/Seed/Nut: When ripe, the seeds are brown to brownish green, about 1/2 inch long, wide, and 1/3 inch across, and shaped like cheese wheels. Usually hairless, the nutlets have a sharp angle between the dorsal and lateral surfaces.

Look-a-likes: Common mallow can be confused with a common Carolina geranium. Geranium weed leaves, however, are more deeply divided.

Caution: The seeds can be toxic if eaten in large quantities but are otherwise safe and tasty.

Culinary Uses: The seeds can be eaten raw as snacks. You can cook the leaves and prepare them like spinach or other greens. You can also eat or even pickle the flowers.

Medicinal Uses: In medieval herbal medicine, common mallow was used as a cure-all, like astringents, diuretics, emollients, expectorants, laxatives, and salves. The demulcent properties make it valuable as a poultice for bruises, inflammations, insect bites, etc. or ingested for respiratory and digestive problems. Combined with eucalyptus, it is a helpful remedy for coughs and other chest ailments.

Fun/Historical Fact: The original ingredient in marshmallows is Althaea officinalis or Marsh Mallow, one species in this family.

Pet Toxicity: Low toxicity has been reported, but only when consumed in large quantities.

M ugwort
Artemisia vulgaris [AR-TEM-EE-zee-ah vul-GAIR-iss]

Common Mugwort is abundant and easy to forage. It is a part of the **Asteraceae** (daisy) family. It goes by several names: Felon Herb, St. John's Plant, Chrysanthemum Weed, Wild Wormwood, Old Uncle Henry, Sailor's Tobacco, Maiden Wort, and Chinese Honeysuckle. It can be used for food and medicine alike.

Mugwort grows readily near water, like rivers and streams. It's also found on roadsides and in wastelands.

Identify:

GROWTH/SIZE: A **herbaceous perennial** plant can reach up to 6 feet tall and be just as wide.

BARK/STEM/ROOT: The stems are purple-brown, angular, furrowed, and largely hairless, except for the flowering stems.

LEAF: It has **elliptic, oblong,** and deeply lobed **basal** leaves. The leaves are lobed **pinnately** or **bipinnately** and are 4 inches long and 2.5 inches wide. Leaf margins can be **serrated**, and the underside can be pale with hairs.

FLOWER - blooms from July to October with yellowish-green to reddish-brown flowerheads, each with rayless florets and thread-like *pistils*. A lot of them are egg-shaped and stand erect to drooping.

FRUIT/SEED/NUT: An *achene* is small and lightweight, and the wind blows it. Rather than spreading through seeds, it spreads through vegetative expansion and *anthropogenic* dispersal of root *rhizomes*.

Look-a-likes: This plant should be collected carefully because the leaves can look like Monkshood.

Caution: If harvested in waste areas, ensure it hasn't been sprayed with herbicides.

Culinary Uses: Edible parts of the plant are young shoots, flower buds, flowers, stems, and leaves. Mugwort has a long history in the culinary world. It has a distinctive musty herbal fragrance and a slightly bitter flavor. A dried version of this spice is commonly used for seasoning meats. The leaves can be cooked in soups or eaten fresh in salads, and it has also been used in teas and alcoholic drinks and was used before hops when brewing beer.

Medicinal Uses: Throughout history, there have been numerous traditional uses of mugwort in various parts of the world. In modern times, mugwort is taken orally to treat digestive problems, irregular menstruation, and high blood pressure. Additionally, it is promoted as a sedative, laxative, and liver tonic.

Fun Facts: In Medieval Europe, mugwort was used to help fatigue and keep moths out of gardens.

In Ukrainian, Mugwort is called Chornobyl, meaning "Black Stalk"; the city got its name from this plant.

In China, it is used in cuisine and can be tracked back to 3 B.C. through poets such as Su Shi in the 11th century.

The goose is a delicacy in Germany, and mugwort is used to season the bird.

Pet Toxicity: Mugwort is toxic to dogs. It contains a chemical called terpene, which can cause diarrhea and vomiting. The essential oil also contains thujone, which can affect the nervous system.

Ostrich Fern

Onoclea struthiopteris [ON-OH-KLEE-UH STRUTH-EE-OP-TER-ISS]

Fiddleheads are an unusual edible. They're very young Ostrich ferns, and you usually only have a short time to harvest them. They belong to the *Aspleniaceae* (spleenwort) family. Other names, such as Fiddlehead Fern and Shuttlecock fern, often refer to them.

It is commonly found in wetland areas such as bogs, swamps, and streams. It also grows in moist, shady locations such as woodlands and near the edges of rivers and lakes. It is also cultivated and used as an ornamental plant in gardens and landscapes. It is also considered a valuable food source for wildlife.

Identification: It's a perennial fern species native to North America and parts of Europe.

Growth/Size: A large, robust fern that can grow up to 6 feet tall and 4 feet wide.

Bark/Stem/Root: The stem is typically unbranched and has a green color. It's also covered in a brownish-black, scaly covering that gives it a rough texture and is generally triangular.

Leaf: The fronds are large, feathery, and triangular, and the fertile fronds are shorter and bear tiny, brown spores on the undersides of the leaflets.

99

FLOWER: No flower to speak of.

FRUIT/SEED/NUT: no fruit or seed present.

Look-a-likes: Other, non-edible ferns form fiddleheads as well. Make sure that the fiddlehead is the suitable fern. The fiddleheads must be cooked before eating.

Caution: It's important to note that many ferns are toxic if ingested raw, so cooking fiddleheads before eating them is essential.

Culinary Uses: Remove any papery brown skin and trim away any brown stem ends. Wash the fiddleheads thoroughly, then boil for at least 5 minutes or steam for 10 minutes, ensuring they are thoroughly cooked. You can eat them as they are, fry them, or use them like any other asparagus or broccoli. Use within a week of Harvest or freeze.

Medicinal Uses: Fiddleheads have been used to treat various ailments, such as stomach aches, constipation, and skin irritations. The rhizomes have been used to make a poultice to treat wounds, burns, and skin irritations.

Fun/Historical Fact: Flowering plants did not exist when ferns first appeared in fossil records. That means dinosaurs are younger than them! By more than 100 million years!

Pet Toxicity: Fiddleheads are safe for dogs in small quantities. Fiddleheads are loaded with healthy vitamins and minerals and must be served cooked, as raw fiddleheads can cause vomiting, diarrhea, and food poisoning in dogs. To avoid a choking hazard, feed in small pieces.

Pineapple Weed

Matricaria discoidea [MA-TRI-KARE-EE-A DIS-KO-ID-EE-A]

Pineapple weed, known as Disc Mayweed and Rayless Mayweed, has nothing to do with actual pineapples. Like other plants you've read about, it belongs to the Asteraceae (daisy/sunflower) family. It is, however, easy to spot, tasty, and can be made into a relaxing tea.

It grows readily around walking paths, roadsides, disturbed areas, fences, and meadows.

Identification: Due to its small size, it is often overlooked, but it is a persistent weed that can reproduce easily and spread quickly.

GROWTH/SIZE: This small annual herb grows about 6-12 inches tall.

BARK/STEM/ROOT: The stem is generally thin, upright, green, and slightly hairy.

LEAF: Green leaf blades measure 1-2 inches long. The leaves are deeply lobed and feathery, making them look delicate and lacy. An alternate pattern of leaves is arranged on the stem. Leaves do not have small leaflets, so they are simple.

FLOWER: The flowers are small, yellow, and arranged in a dense, round, disk-like head, giving the plant its common name. The flowers are about 1/4 inch wide, with a yellow disk-shaped receptacle and yellow ray florets. The disk comprises many

101

small, tubular disk florets, each with five protruding stamens. The flowers bloom in the summer and early fall.

FRUIT/SEED/NUT: it becomes a brown head of seeds without hair tufts.

Look-a-likes: It has a distinctive appearance that makes them relatively easy to identify. However, it can be mistaken for other similar-looking plants, such as German chamomile (Matricaria chamomilla), stinking chamomile (Anthemis cotula), or ox-eye daisy (Leucanthemum vulgare). These plants are closely related and have similar-looking flowers, leaves, and growth habits.

Caution: Though generally safe for most people to consume or use topically, some individuals may be allergic or sensitive to it, causing skin irritation or allergic reactions. It is also possible that consuming large amounts of the plant could cause stomach upset or other symptoms.

Culinary Uses: They are edible and are used in salads and herbal tea. Most people use fresh or dried flowers to make tea. Steep them in boiling water for 4-5 minutes and enjoy.

Medicinal Uses: Medical uses of pineapple weed have included treating gastrointestinal upsets, infected sores, fevers, and anemia caused by pregnancy.

Fun/Historical Fact: They are hermaphrodites, meaning each flower has male and female reproductive organs.

Pet Toxicity: Given moderation, pineapple weed is not toxic for your dog.

Pink Wood Sorrel

Oxalis articulata [OKS-AL-ISS AR-TIK-YOO-LAH-TUH]

Wood Sorrel has a sour and tangy taste and has been used for culinary purposes for centuries. It's a part of the ***Oxalidaceae*** (wood sorrel) family. Common names are Oxalis, Pink Oxalis, and Pink Wood Sorrel. In addition to being used as a potted plant, it is also used as a perennial border plant.

Wood sorrel grows readily in partial shade. It's common in yards, gardens, grasslands, and parks.

Identification: This perennial is dense and mounded, deciduous, and has rhizomes.

GROWTH/SIZE: It commonly grows in clumps about 8 inches tall and 8 inches wide.

BARK/STEM/ROOT: There is no stem to speak of.

LEAF: Plants have compound, obovate leaves, and notch-topped leaves erect to spread. Each leaf has three clover-shaped leaflets, incised triangular, whole, bright green, or burgundy, that fold down at night. The petioles are long and slender.

FLOWER: Various colors are available, including pink, white, magenta, and yellow. The foliage of this plant can partially conceal the flowers. The petals, partially fused at the base of the flower, can grow up to an inch in size. In each flower, there are two whorls of five stamens. The inflorescence is an umbel with a long pedicel and a diameter of up to 3 inches. A continuous flowering season occurs from early spring to the first frost, and then it goes dormant. In the shade, the flowers roll up into a tube-like shape.

Fruit/Seed/Nut: When ripe, fruits eject seeds from their fleshy capsules.

Look-a-likes: It looks similar to clover, which isn't toxic but can cause bloating.

Caution: Wood sorrel contains oxalic acid, which gives it a sour flavor. Unfortunately, eating large amounts of oxalic acid can be harmful, and it's recommended not to eat it if you have certain medical conditions. However, eating enough wood sorrel to worry about is challenging in most cases. Spinach and broccoli also contain oxalic acid.

Culinary Uses: You can eat the leaves, flowers, and young seed pods. Use it the same day you harvest it. It's great raw in salads, but you can cook it to make tea.

Medicinal Uses: If you use Oxalis as a remedy, you should exercise MODERATION. The herb may reduce the discomfort of fevers when brewed with one ounce of herb to one pint of water. In small doses of no more than two fluid ounces per day, Oxalis may help relieve urinary tract infections. Gargling with it has been effective in eliminating mouth ulcers and sores. When made into an ointment, it can be used externally to treat cuts, scrapes, rashes, and skin infections. Extracts of oxalate from the leaves have been shown to have anti-fungal properties.

Fun/Historical Fact: Heed the warnings above but know that a wide range of foods contains oxalic acid naturally in small amounts, such as rhubarb, spinach, mustard greens, poppy seeds, sweet potatoes, cabbage, pumpkin, strawberries, mangoes, tomatoes, parsnips.

Pet Toxicity: Sorrel contains high levels of insoluble calcium oxalates, which are toxic to dogs. Even small amounts of sorrel can irritate a dog's mouth, throat, esophagus, and gastrointestinal tract.

P lantain (Greater)

Plantago major [PLAN-TA-GO MAY-JOR]

Plantains were first described in the "Materia Medica" by a Greek botanist, Pedanius Dioscorides (40-90 AD). It's been used for culinary and medicinal purposes for years and is sometimes called "nature's band-aid." It is a part of the *Plantaginaceae* (plantain) family and has many other names. You may recognize a few: Cart Track Plant, Cuckoo's bread, Doorweed, Whiteman's-foot, and Ripple Grass.

Plantain grows everywhere. You might even have some in your backyard. Plantains are found in forests, meadows, fields, wastelands, and roadsides. This plant thrives in disturbed or compacted soil and can withstand repeated trampling.

Identification: It is an herbaceous, flowering, perennial plant.

GROWTH/SIZE: It can grow up to 12 inches in diameter.

BARK/STEM/ROOT: Small, inconspicuous flowers emerge on erect, leafless stems less than 12 inches tall and unbranched.

LEAF: Broadly lance-shaped or egg-shaped leaves with an acute apex form a rosette. They range in size from 2 to 8 inches in length and 2 to 4 inches in width. If a leaf is pulled from the plant, a petiole will show several prominent, stringy veins at its base. There is a medium green color on the upper surface of each blade, and it is

105

glabrous to sparsely canescent. On the lower surface, light green veins are finely pubescent.

FLOWER: Usually appearing between April and September, the flowers are inconspicuous greenish-brown, and the stamens range from white to purple. From the center of the plant, a narrow cylindrical spike forms a dense cluster of greenish flowers. Seeds form all along the stem.

FRUIT/SEED/NUT: Each capsule has two equal segments, containing six to twenty brown, glossy, ridged seeds. Several animals eat the seeds. Each plant produces up to 20,000 tiny, bitter, oval-shaped seeds.

Look-a-likes: Plantains do not have toxic look-a-likes.

Caution: Beware that they have not been sprayed with pesticides.

Culinary Uses: Plantain is often used to create a quick poultice to treat bug bites or minor wounds. You can also eat and use it as you would kale or other bitter greens.

Medicinal Uses: Plantain is multi-functional regarding injuries and has been labeled the Band-Aid plant. It is used to treat eye ailments, including choroid disease, day blindness, conjunctivitis, and sore eyes, by juicing the leaves. A leaf extract reduces lung and pleural lesions when taken orally with honey. It treats upper and lower gastrointestinal bleeding, dysentery, hemorrhoids, stomachaches, intestinal ulcers, and constipation by eating the leaf extract and baking the leaves with salt and vinegar. Alternatively, it can be used as an enema. This plant's seed or root extract has been used as a liver tonic and in obstructive liver and spleen diseases. In localized applications, it relieves bladder and kidney pain, urinary retention, and problems associated with urinary retention. Lastly, sprinkling plant powder on the wound or mixing plaster with salt treats various types of injuries and skin disorders, like deep wounds, chronic wounds, malignant wounds, fire burns, and progressive blisters.

Fun/Historical Fact: The plantain is not the same as the banana fruit called plantain.

Pet Toxicity: They can have all parts of the plantain. It can reduce bladder, kidney, and urinary tract inflammation. It can help with constipation OR diarrhea depending on whether you feed the seeds and husks wet or dry.

Purple Deadnettle

lamium purpureum [LAY-mee-um pur-PUR-ee-um]

It is named for its leaves, which resemble stinging nettle (*Urtica*) but lack stings since they are "dead." It is a part of the *Lamiaceae* (mint or deadnettle) family and goes by these common names: Purple Archangel, Red Dead Nettle, and Velikdenche.

It prefers disturbed areas, such as footpaths, roadsides, and fields. It may even be in your backyard.

Identification: Purple dead nettle is an invaluable plant for pollinators. Its flowers attract bees and provide pollen that is an undyed red color.

GROWTH/SIZE: Can reach 8-10 inches tall.

BARK/STEM/ROOT: Stems are square and green.

LEAF: Overlapping heart-shaped leaves are often purple, with greenish undersides and hairy upper surfaces. The leaf margins are wavy to serrated, and the petioles are short.

FLOWER: The purple flowers have a hooded top petal and two lips on the lower portion. Produced throughout the year, they are *sessile* and grow in *whorls* in the axils of the leaves.

Fruit/Seed/Nut: A purple deadnettle plant produces 600 seeds but can have 27,000 when it's not competing with other plants for space.

Look-a-likes: It doesn't have any toxic look-a-likes, but in many places, it grows with Henbit Dead-nettle (*Lamium amplexicaule*), which is easily confused with purple deadnettle due to its similar leaves and bright purple flowers. Don't worry; they are both edible.

Caution: Those who eat generous amounts of dead nettle leaves may experience mild laxative effects. Consumption of too much herbal tea can cause diarrhea.

Culinary Uses: The purple tops are slightly sweet, and the leaves are highly nutritious. It's usually used as a herb or garnish mixed with other greens.

Medicinal Uses: Purple deadnettle can be enjoyed internally and externally. It has been used for centuries to create salves, tinctures, and teas to treat various injuries or illnesses. It is an excellent source of vitamins A, C, and K, fiber, iron, and bioflavonoids. These leaves also have anti-inflammatory, antibacterial, and anti-fungal properties and are diuretic, astringent, diaphoretic, and purgative. Herbal remedies containing dead nettle have traditionally been used for treating kidney disease, seasonal allergies, chills, and common colds. In addition to boosting the immune system, consumption of this edible can also help combat bacterial infections. Additionally, the leaves can be used to create a poultice that can be used externally to heal cuts, burns, and bruises.

Fun/Historical Fact: Many myths and folklore stories surround this ancient plant. Traditionally, it has been used in magical ceremonies to promote happiness, security, and grounding. Those who wield this early-blooming plant are said to gain the same power it offers.

Pet Toxicity: No evidence of toxicity or beneficial uses in pets exists.

P urslane

Portulaca oleracea [POR-TEW-LAK-uh AWL-LUR-RAY-SEE-uh]

Purslane is another weed that's common throughout North America and Eurasia. Some people deliberately cultivate it, but once you know how to spot it, you can quickly harvest it from the wild. It is a part of the *Portulacaceae* (purslane) family. It goes by these other names: Garden Purslane, Little Hogweed, Moss Rose, Pigweed, Portulaca, Red Root, Rock Moss, Verdolaga, and Wild Portulaca.

Purslane grows in wastelands and disturbed areas, such as gravelly soil and cracks in the sidewalk.

Identification: Its origin is obscure, but Purslane is regarded as one of the ten most noxious weeds worldwide. It is generally considered a native of western Asia or Europe. Still, evidence suggests it may have been here before European settlement.

GROWTH/SIZE: In the wild, the plant may reach 16 inches in height and form dense mats up to 20 inches across.

BARK/STEM/ROOT: Stems are usually prostrate, smooth, and straight. Their shape is round, thick, and succulent. Their color ranges from light green to reddish brown. There are multiple branches on each stem, creating circular mats.

LEAF: An oval leaf with smooth, fleshy edges that tends to cluster at the joints and stem ends. They grow 1-3 inches in length, and it's not uncommon for the leaves to turn reddish-purple under bright sunlight. In the early stages of growth, the undersides of young leaves have a maroon tint.

FLOWER: A 1/4-inch-long yellow flower with five heart-shaped petals can appear at any time of the year. Their opening occurs only in the morning and is found in the cluster of leaves at the stem's end.

FRUIT/SEED/NUT: One plant can develop up to 193,000 seeds. Once split open, the egg-shaped capsule scatters tiny black, shiny seeds.

Look-a-likes: As mentioned before, spurges are the closest toxic look-alike to Purslane. The easiest way to tell the difference is to look for fleshy, succulent leaves. Spurges have flatter leaves and exude white latex when broken.

Caution: Contains oxalates that can be toxic if eaten in high amounts.

Culinary Uses: Immerse your collected Purslane in water to eliminate seeds and dirt. Get rid of thick stems and store them in the refrigerator. It has a mild, lemony flavor with a nice crunch. You can eat it raw in salads and sandwiches or steam it as a side dish. It also makes a delicious soup.

Medicinal Uses: Many countries use purslane as folk medicine to reduce fevers, treat infections, eliminate parasites, etc. The main pharmacological effects of this plant include its antibacterial activity, anti-ulcerogenic, anti-inflammatory, antioxidant, and wound-healing properties.

Fun/Historical Fact: Purslane is very nutritious, with vitamins A, B, and C. They're also high in antioxidants, potassium, magnesium, and calcium. Its the highest recorded levels of omega-3 fatty acids of any land-based plant. Omega-3 fatty acids help to support healthy arteries and can help prevent strokes, heart attacks, and other forms of heart disease. They have five times more omega-3 fatty acids than spinach.

Pet Toxicity: Purslane is toxic to your pup and can cause a metabolic imbalance. Some signs of metabolic imbalance are hypersalivation, weakness, and tremors. If your dog exhibits these symptoms, it could be at risk for kidney failure.

S assafras

Sassafras albidum [SAS-ah-fras AL-bih-dum]

Sassafras is traditionally used for medicinal, culinary, and aromatic purposes. People most commonly harvest leaves, bark, and roots. It is part of the **Lauraceae** (laurel) family. Here are a few other names it's known by: Cinnamon Wood, Mitten Tree, and White Sassafras

This tree prefers full sun and is commonly found in wooded areas and fields. It thrives in acidic, sandy soil.

Identification: A spicy and aromatic flavor can be found in all parts of this plant. In addition, the roots are thick and fleshy, frequently producing root sprouts capable of growing into new trees.

Growth/Size: A medium-sized deciduous tree growing 49–66 feet tall with a canopy 39 feet wide.

Bark/Stem/Root: When mature, it has a deeply furrowed, dark reddish-brown bark on a trunk that can expand to 24 inches in diameter.

Leaf: The leaves grow alternately on the branches reaching up to 6 inches long and 4 inches wide. They may or may not be lobed.

FLOWER: The flowers appear in loose, drooping *racemes* up to 2 inches long in early spring. The flowers are yellow and greenish-yellow, with five or six *tepals*. Male and female flowers are often found on separate trees, and male flowers have nine *stamens*. In contrast, females have six *staminodes* (*aborted stamens*).

FRUIT/SEED/NUT: A single seed is contained within the dark blue-black drupe, borne on a red fleshy club-shaped pedicel 3/4 inch long. The fruit ripens in late summer, and birds disperse the seeds.

Look-a-likes: Though only as a seedling, the mulberry has leaves that resemble those of the sassafras tree. After maturing, the mulberry tree berries are the easiest way to distinguish the two.

Caution: Only harvest what you need, and don't cause undue damage to the tree, especially if you're gathering the roots. Consuming large amounts of sassafras oil may cause health problems. Don't consume sassafras if you're pregnant.

Culinary Uses: You can steep the root or dried bark in boiling water to make sassafras tea. The leaves can be dried and ground to make file seasoning, used in Creole cuisine to thicken sauces.

Medicinal Uses: Some Native American tribes used sassafras leaves to treat wounds by rubbing them directly on the wound. The roots and berries were made into tea and used for acne treatment, urinary disorders treatment, and high fever treatment.

Fun/Historical Fact: Leaves and oils have been used in food products, soaps, and fragrances. Wood is used to make furniture and boats.

Pet Toxicity: Sassafras contains safrole, a toxic ingredient that can potentially harm a dog when consumed in large quantities. It can cause liver damage and cancer in dogs.

Staghorn Sumac

Rhus typhina [RHOOS TY-FEE-NAH]

Unlike the infamous Poison Sumac, Staghorn Sumac is perfectly edible and delicious. It's part of the ***Anacardiaceae*** (cashew or sumac) family, so this plant may not be for you if you have a nut allergy. It has a bright, tart flavor and a hint of bitterness.

Sumac grows on roadsides and at the edges of woods.

Identification: The plant is not poisonous, but its suckers cause it to spread like a weed. If you are lucky enough to have this growing in your yard, you can rejuvenate your sumac by cutting leggy plants to the ground every few years.

GROWTH/SIZE: It grows up to 25 feet tall and wide and spreads like a weed.

BARK/STEM/ROOT: Branches of young trees are covered with reddish-brown hairs similar to the velvet covering stag horns, hence the common name.

LEAF: In the fall, the medium green leaves turn attractive shades of scarlet, yellow, and orange. There are 11-31 lanceolate leaflets with serrate margins on alternate 16-24 inch leaves.

FLOWER: This plant blooms with showy white blossoms in spring and summer. The male and female flowers are on separate trees, and the panicles grow from 4 to 8 inches tall with 1/4" greenish-white petals.

Fruit/Seed/Nut: A female plant has only fruit. The cluster contains hairy, round drupes that ripen bright red in summer and turn dark red in winter.

Look-a-like: Poison sumac will irritate your skin when you touch it. Thankfully, these berries are white or green, so you can differentiate between them when they're ripe.

Culinary Uses: Watch for the Staghorn sumac berries starting in late July or early August. You can use scissors to cut off sumac berry heads once the berries turn a deep red. You can use some fresh to make tea by steeping them in boiling water for at least 30 minutes or as a fantastic sumac version of lemonade by crushing 6-8 heads in a bowl or pitcher and topping with cold water. After an hour, strain them through cheesecloth and add honey, maple syrup, or sugar to taste. The remaining harvest can be dehydrated in an air dehydrator or oven at a low temperature and then jarred for future use.

Caution: Some people may develop a skin rash after coming into contact with the sap of this species. Also, as it is a member of the cashew family, anyone with a sensitivity to nuts may want to avoid it.

Medicinal Uses: Astringents such as Staghorn Sumac are wonderful when soft tissues lack structure or are damp. Therefore, it is suitable as a wash for acne or a mouth rinse for soft, bleeding gums. The cream helps tone or tighten skin, reducing inflammation and removing oil.

Fun/Historical Fact: Staghorn has a deep history related to magic in several different cultures. The nahikàï is a wand used in a Navajo shaman healing ceremony. A Sumac branch 3 feet long and about ½" thick. Eagle-down feathers are attached to the end of the wand and burned off as part of the ceremony.

Beekeepers love to use dried Staghorn Sumac in their smokers. It smolders nicely and produces a very caring smoke.

Pet Toxicity: Non-toxic to your pup.

Watercress
Nasturtium officinale [Nas-tur-tium of-fic-i-nale]

Watercress is a bright, peppery plant that most people find familiar. It is a member of the **Brassicaceae** (mustard or cabbage) family. It has several other names like Common Nasturtium, Garden Nasturtium, Indian Cress, Mexican Cress, Nose-Tweaker, Nose-Twister, and Peruvian Cress.

Watercress can be found in water, as its name suggests. Look for cold, alkaline waters, like springs, spring runs, and streams.

Identification: Watercress is a perennial herb that grows in aquatic or semiaquatic environments. Humans have consumed this leaf vegetable for thousands of years.

GROWTH/SIZE: It grows from 4 to 10 inches high.

BARK/STEM/ROOT: Roots are found at succulent, hollow, branched stem nodes.

LEAF: You can locate it by its alternate, pinnately compound leaves. They're around 1.5 to 6.5 inches long and have 2 to 8 oval-shaped leaflets in opposite pairs, ending in a larger leaflet. Each leaflet has wavy edges.

FLOWER: The blossoms are seen from June to September and are tiny and white, with four petals and yellow stamens.

Fruit/Seed/Nut: The fruit is a slender pod between 3/8 and 1 inch long, slightly curved, ascending to spreading, and having a short, abrupt beak at the tip. A pair of rows of oval, reddish-brown seeds appear when mature.

Look-a-likes: In terms of look-a-likes, watercress isn't much of a threat, but be sure that the water source you are foraging from is clean and untainted.

Caution: Wild harvesting should be done with some care. Using raw plants grown in water draining from fields where animals, primarily sheep, graze is not recommended. This is because it may be infected with the liver fluke parasite. Cooking the leaves will destroy any parasites, and the plant will be safe to consume.

Culinary Uses: Watercress is delicious and nutritious when eaten raw, with a peppery taste similar to mustard greens. When cooked, watercress loses both its flavor and nutritional value. Still, it adds a unique flavor and texture to soups, stews, and stir-fries.

Medicinal Uses: It is used in traditional medicine to treat hypercholesterolemia, hyperglycemia, hypertension, arthritis, bronchitis, diuresis, toothaches, and scurvy. In addition to acting as an antiestrogenic, it can be used as a nutritional supplement.

Fun/Historical Fact: Watercress is considered an incredibly nutritious superfood. Most notably, it has a large amount of vitamin K and high levels of vitamins C and A. It's also a good source of vitamin B6.

Pet Toxicity: Watercress itself is non-toxic for your pup; however, because it grows in the water, it can soak up toxins and bacteria from the water, which can be toxic.

Wild Garlic
Allium canadense [AL-ee-um ka-na-DEN-see]

Field garlic is a common allium and invasive weed, sometimes known as ramsons, cowleekes, cows' leek, crow garlic, wild garlic, or onion grass. It belongs to the *Amaryllidaceae* (amaryllis) family. You can eat every part of the plant, from the bulb to the leaves and flowers.

Field garlic grows abundantly in most places, including backyards, woodland edges, wastelands, and fields.

Identification: There is a strong onion smell and taste in the plant.

GROWTH/SIZE: A mature plant has about 18 inches tall. In a favorable location, it can spread quite freely.

BARK/STEM/ROOT: It emerges from the ground with stalks about the same height as the leaves or slightly higher. The stalks are terete (round in cross-section) rather than flat and are held rigidly upright.

LEAF: It has narrow, grass-like leaves that reach 8-12 inches in height and sprout from the stem's base. It has erect to semi-erect leaves that tend to be linear, flat, and slightly arched; they are light to medium green and glabrous. It sets underground bulbs that are no bigger than pearl onions and are covered in brown fibers.

FLOWER: The flowers typically appear in the form of a dome-shaped cluster, pink or white, that looks like a star. There are male and female organs in the flowers, which are pollinated by American bees (not honeybees) and other insects. Between May and June, it is usually in full bloom.

FRUIT/SEED/NUT: Bulblets may replace some or all of these flowers. The seed capsules contain several tiny seeds that range in color from dark brown to coppery.

Look-a-like: Crow garlic, *allium vineale,* is similar but has a strong garlic flavor.

Caution: There are no known cautions for wild garlic unless you don't like onions.

Culinary Uses: Young field garlic can be used the same way as chives. Once the bulbs have matured, you can use them like garlic cloves.

Medicinal Uses: The tincture can prevent worms and colic in children and treat croup. In addition to reducing blood cholesterol levels, they are a tonic for the digestive system. They also strengthen the circulatory system when added to the diet regularly.

Fun/Historical Fact: An insect bite or sting can be treated with a crushed bulb in traditional medicine.

Pet Toxicity: In large quantities, garlic (and onions, chives, etc.) is very toxic for dogs. It can cause diarrhea, vomiting, weakness, and, eventually, collapse.

Wild Ramp
Allium tricoccum [AL-ee-um try-KOK-um]

Wild ramps have a fantastic garlicky-onion flavor, and the leaves shine. Like truffles, they're typically foraged, giving them an air of mystery. They are a part of the *Amaryllidaceae* (amaryllis) family. They are known as Wild Leeks, Spring onions, or Ramsoms and are an increasingly popular wild edible.

You can find them as ground cover in dense deciduous forests.

Identification: Many ramps grow close together, strongly rooted beneath the soil's surface.

Growth/Size: A perennial herbaceous monocot that is bulbous in appearance and grows 8-12 inches tall.

Bark/Stem/Root: The bulbs are white and surrounded by a brownish-to-grayish sheath. There is one flowering stem per cluster of bulbs. Typically, flowering occurs after the leaves have died back. The flowers are usually arranged into an umbel with an erect scape measuring 4-16 inches long. Inflorescences consist of two ovate bracts that enclose blooms before they open. Flowering stems persist after fruiting.

Leaf: Its leaves are broad, flat, smooth, and light green, with narrow petioles, and its lower stems have deep purple or burgundy tints.

FLOWER: The flowering period occurs between June and August. Usually, the flower's tepals are white, cream, or yellowish. The stamens have widened bases, and the filaments of the stamens are inserted into the flower's corolla.

FRUIT/SEED/NUT: Three-lobed, three-valved green fruit is produced after flowering and fertilization. Its seeds are shiny, round, and black.

Look-a-likes: Lily of the Valley and False hellebore are examples of toxic look-a-likes for wild ramps. When in doubt, smell the plant. It should smell strongly of onion or garlic, like other edible alliums.

Caution: none known

Culinary Uses: While you can eat the stems and bulbs, most people focus on the leaves. The leaves are delicious, and you can use them as you would onions, leeks, or garlic. You can freeze the bulbs, but the leaves should be refrigerated because they don't freeze well. Use them as quickly as you can. The most common way to prepare ramps in southern Appalachia is to fry them with potatoes in bacon fat or scramble them with eggs, bacon, and pinto beans. As a substitute for onions and garlic, ramps can also be pickled and used in soups.

Medicinal Uses: It was used by the Cherokee as a spring tonic for colds and to treat croup. The juice from the plant was warmed and used to treat earaches; a decoction was taken as an emetic.

Fun/Historical Fact: Each year, Elkins, West Virginia, hosts the "Ramps and Rails Festival" during the last weekend in April, which features a cook-off and ramp-eating contests. In Whitetop, Virginia, the Mount Rogers Volunteer Fire Department holds its annual ramp festival the third weekend in May. It features food and fun for everyone, and The Wild Ramp, an indoor farmers market, hosts "Stink Fest," an annual ramp festival in Huntington, West Virginia.

Pet Toxicity: The leek is one type of vegetable responsible for dog poisoning, similar to its relatives, the onion, garlic, and chives. Even a tiny portion of leeks is dangerous for your dog and will cause damage to the red blood cells, ultimately resulting in hemolytic anemia.

Y ellow Sweetclover

Melilotus officinalis [MEL-I-LO-TUS OF-FIS-IN-AY-LIS]

Yellow sweetclover was brought to North America as a forage crop and rapidly escaped cultivation. The plant proliferates following a burn and likes to be around fire. It is part of the *Fabaceae* (legume) family. It has several different names: yellow melilot, ribbed melilot, and common melilot. It's very nutritious and is exceptionally high in protein. In a given year, honey bee hives living near sweet clover can produce 200 pounds of honey.

Yellow Sweet Clover is common in fields, meadows, pastures, roadsides, and wastelands.

Identification: Yellow Sweet clover is a biennial plant and is far easier to spot in its second year of growth.

GROWTH/SIZE: It grows on tall stems about 2-5 feet tall in the second year.

BARK/STEM/ROOT: They have ridged or grooved stems, are primarily hairless, and are usually green or red.

LEAF: On a stalk about an inch long, leaves are compounded in groups of three. The leaflets measure 1/2 to 1 inch long and 1/4 to 1/2 inch across. The tips are rounded, the edges have tiny teeth, and the stalks are short. Leaflets can have an

121

oval or elliptical shape or taper to a narrow base, with the widest point at the tip. Depending on the light, the color may appear blue-green or gray-green.

FLOWER: Branching stems from the leaf axis are adorned with spike-like racemes up to six inches long with yellow flowers. Each flower has five parts about 1/4 inch long. It is not uncommon for large plants to take on a bushy appearance with many yellow flowers scattered throughout. Late spring and early fall is the blooming season.

FRUIT/SEED/NUT: In place of each flower, a small pod with a flattened beak contains 1-2 seeds. Transverse ridges are typically curved on each side. Tannish yellow seeds are ovoid-reniform in shape and somewhat flattened.

Look-a-likes: White Sweet Clover (*Melilotus alba*) starts blooming a few weeks after the Yellow and is a slightly larger plant. Except for the flower color and bloom time, they are nearly identical.

Caution: Eating large amounts of sweet clover may cause nausea. Pregnant women should avoid it, as it contains dicoumarol. This naturally occurring anticoagulant drug depletes stores of vitamin K in the body and has been linked to gestational issues.

Culinary Uses: Use young leaves as bitter salad greens. Most people use the plant for tea or syrup.

Medicinal Uses: Sweet clover contains ingredients that can thin the blood and help wounds heal. It has been used as a diuretic. Also, it relieves symptoms of poor blood circulation, including leg pain and heaviness, night cramps, itchiness, varicose veins, and fluid retention (edema). Some people apply sweet clover directly to the skin for bruises.

Fun/Historical Fact: Sweet clover was an important green manure crop before World War II. Its ability to grow rapidly and fix nitrogen made it an ideal green manure. Plowing under sweet clover residue increases soil nitrogen content when used for green manure compared to harvesting top growth for forage.

Pet Toxicity: Though the plant itself isn't toxic, it can develop mold that can be fatal and, of course, like any other plant classified as a weed, has the potential to be deadly because of commercial weed killers.

PAY IT FORWARD!

"The greatest gifts are not wrapped in paper but in love and the beauty of nature." -
Anonymous.

Picture this: someone's standing in the middle of the wilderness, surrounded by the raw beauty of nature. But there's a tiny hiccup - they're a tad unsure which of the green wonders before them might serve as a delicious snack or which might send them on an unplanned trip to the ER. Now, what if YOUR review could be the deciding factor that guides them on this journey? Leaving a review isn't just a simple clickety-clack of your keyboard. Nope! It's a chance to share your wisdom, your "Ah-ha!" moments, and even your "Oops, shouldn't have eaten that" tales. By jotting down your thoughts, you're crafting a lighthouse for fellow enthusiasts, helping them navigate the vast ocean of edible greens.

Why We Need YOU!

We're reaching out with a heartfelt plea: could you spare a few moments to leave an honest review? Your words will be the torch that lights up another enthusiast's path.

How to Review:

- Just scan the QR code below:

- Pour your heart out! Let us know what you loved and learned and any tips you might have.

- Hit "Submit," and voilà, the review is done! It only takes 30 seconds to help others benefit.

The Ripple Effect

Every keystroke, every word, creates a ripple. By sharing your experiences, you're not just adding to a digital platform but making a real, tangible impact in some-one's life. Your review could catalyze someone's passion or help a novice avoid a potentially prickly situation.

With gratitude and a green thumbs-up, Shannon Warner

PART FIVE
TREES AND NUTS

American Beech

Fagus grandifolia [FAG-us GRAN-DIH-FOH-lee-uh]

Beechnuts are sweet and delicious. The American Beech is a part of the *Fagaceae* (beech) family. Other common names for this tree include Beechnut Tree, Red Beech, Ridge Beech, and White Beech. In documented history, the oldest tree dates back 246 years.

Beech trees can be found in hardwood forests and prefers moist, well-drained soil. You can usually find them with maple trees.

Identification: American beech trees only produce significant amounts of nuts once they are about 40 years old. It takes 60 years for large crops to be grown.

GROWTH/SIZE: The height of this large deciduous tree can range from 52 to 115 feet.

BARK/STEM/ROOT: Their bark is distinctively smooth, thin, and gray. The pattern appears zigzag-like, grayish, and shiny.

LEAF: It has simple, alternate, ovate-oblong leaves 2 to 5 inches long, with a tapering tip, and are coarsely serrated. The leaves are greenish-brown and glossy on the top and lighter green on the bottom.

FLOWER: American beech blooms with *monoecious* yellowish-green flowers from

March to May. It forms large globular clusters of drooping, long-stemmed male flowers and short spikes of female flowers.

Fruit/Seed/Nut: Two or three prickly husks remain on the tree after the nut has fallen, each approximately 3/4 inches long. September and October is the time when beechnuts ripen and become edible. The nuts drop to the ground in fall, typically around the first frost. If the beechnut shell has collapsed in on itself, or if there's a hole in the surface, it will likely be empty.

Look-a-likes: The European beechnut is edible but bitter. European beech trees resemble American beeches but have darker grey bark and shorter leaves.

Caution: none known

Culinary Uses: Young leaves can be eaten raw or cooked as a herb. The leaves have a mild flavor but quickly become tough, so only use the youngest leaves. Despite their small size, the seeds have a lot of sweetness and nutrition. In addition to being rich in oil, they also contain up to 22% protein. You can make bread, cakes, or biscuits by drying and grinding them into a powder. Germinated seeds are safe to eat raw. They are crunchy, sweet, and nutty. Roasted seeds can be used as a substitute for coffee. The bark can be dried and ground into a powder and used as a thickener in soups or mixed with cereal when making bread.

Medicinal Uses: In treating frostbite, burns, poison ivy rash, and other skin conditions, boiled leaves have been used as a wash and poultice. Lung ailments have been treated with a tea made from the bark.

Fun Facts: Beechwood makes flooring, furniture, veneer plywood, and railroad ties. It is a favored wood for fuel because of its high density and good burning qualities. Coal tar made from beech wood protects the wood from rotting.

Pet Toxicity: Beechnuts are toxic for your pup. Dogs are prone to beech tree poisoning because they like the shape of the husk, where the most potent concentration of tannins is found. Symptoms include nausea, vomiting, diarrhea, abdominal pain, fatigue, and dilated pupils.

A merican Hazelnut

Corylus americana [KOR-EE-LUS A-MER-IH-KAY-NA]

Several grocery stores sell hazelnuts, but you can often find them in the wild. Also known as filberts or cobnuts, wild hazelnuts are usually smaller than commercial varieties. It belongs to the **Betulaceae** (birch) family. I

Hazel trees usually grow in woodland, scrubland, and near thickets.

Identification: Hazelnuts grow on large shrubs or small trees.

GROWTH/SIZE: The tree can grow 10-15 feet tall and 8-15 feet wide.

BARK/STEM/ROOT: The bark is gray and smooth in young branches, while it becomes rougher in older branches and trunks.

LEAF: Its dark green leaves measure up to five inches long and three inches wide. They are oval to elliptical with doubly serrated margins and sparse hairs. Its lower surface is lighter green and dotted with short, stiff hairs. There are several fall colors, from vibrant yellow-red to dull yellow-green.

FLOWER: Flowers of both genders are found on the same plant. Female flowers bloom in clusters from a swollen bud surrounded by protective bracts, only their red stigmata showing beyond. Catkins with yellow to yellow-brown color are the more showy flowers of the male plant. Early spring and winter are the best seasons for blooming.

Fruit/Seed/Nut: As the female flowers mature, they develop into green nuts enclosed by two protective bracts that turn brown when ripe. Nuts are 1/2 inch in size. The nuts can be gathered in the fall, but you're competing with squirrels, who usually get there first. You can harvest them early when they're still green and let them ripen at home.

Look-a-like: Hazelnuts are only edible once fully ripe and slightly dried. The papery outer covering should pull back from the nut before you eat it.

Caution: Some people are allergic to hazelnuts and have had life-threatening reactions, including breathing difficulties.

Culinary Uses: If you harvest them early, then store them in a warm, dry place to let them ripen. Hazelnuts should be dried quickly after harvest at temperatures between 95°F and 105°F. Drying nuts above 110° can negatively affect their flavor. It is recommended to dry nuts for 72 to 96 hours.

Medicinal Uses: A tea made from the bark is astringent. It was used in the treatment of hives and fevers. A poultice made from the bark is used to close cuts and wounds and treat tumors, old sores, etc.

Fun/Historical Fact: The Chippewa used the inner bark as a dye for blankets, rushes, and more. The tribe also used Hazel to make drumsticks, brooms, and baskets. Combining hazel and white oak roots with the inner bark of chokecherry and the heart of ironwood was used for severe bleeding and lung conditions. The Ojibwa tribes used the bark as a poultice for minor cuts and abrasions and, like the Chippewa, made baskets and brooms from the branches.

Pet Toxicity: Hazelnuts aren't toxic to dogs. They pose a choking hazard to smaller dogs and are not recommended as a treat.

Bitternut Hickory

Carya cordiformis [KAIR-yuh kord-ih-FOR-miss]

Hickory is the wood of choice for tools, bows, and furniture because it's as strong as steel yet still flexible. When used as a heat or cooking source, it burns cleanly and makes a long-lasting fire. The hickories belong to the *Juglandaceae* (walnut) family.

Hickory trees grow in hardwood deciduous forests, or you may find them in fields. Bitternut hickory likes damp earth.

Identification: You can usually identify different hickory species by looking at the bark or leaves.

Growth/Size: Bitternut hickory trees reach around 80 feet tall.

Bark/Stem/Root: There is a faint yellow tinge on the trunk's granite gray bark. Although it is less rough than most hickories, it develops narrow, plate-like scales as it ages. In the beginning, the rugged bark is smooth.

Leaf: Five to nine long, oval, toothed leaflets are 6 to 10 inches long, with a yellow-green top and a lighter bottom. On the underside of the veins, there is a slight pubescence.

Flower: Both male and female flowers are produced on the same tree. Greenish-yellow catkins are arranged in three, 3, to 5-inch long clusters, drooping downward from the tips of the previous year's twigs or their bases. Every tiny male flower has several stamens. Three lobes make up the calyx. On the current year's twigs, female flowers appear as short spikes. In female flowers, there are four prominent ridges on the ovary and two styles. They are about an eighth of an inch in diameter. During mid to late spring, flowers bloom for about two weeks.

FRUIT/SEED/NUT: The tree only produces nuts once it is about 30 years old, and they are ready for harvest in October. Four-ribbed nuts have a thin shell, are roughly spherical, and measure about an inch long. There is a bitter taste to the meat of the nut. In addition to having four wings from tip to middle, the husk has yellowish-green, scruffy hairs.

Look-a-like: Bitternuts are bitter and may need to be leached. Buckeye nuts look similar and are toxic. They only have a single nut inside the shell rather than multiple compartments for nut meat.

Caution: Some people are allergic to hazelnuts and have had life-threatening reactions, including breathing difficulties.

Culinary Uses: As with most nuts, you must get through the outer husk and then crack the nut shells to get at the meat within. Bitternuts taste bitter, as their name suggests, so you must roast them and possibly even leech them to make them palatable.

Medicinal Uses: Hickory nuts are high in fatty acids, which prevent constipation by ensuring regular bowel movements. Aside from that, it is also effective in reducing cramps, bloating, and flatulence.

Fun/Historical Fact: Using a hammer to bang on a hickory nut doesn't necessarily result in it splitting open. It would be best to hit it precisely at the right spot to break loose, revealing the meat inside. A membrane separates the shell from the rest of the body. The septum is located here. As a result, the septum divides the kernel, and if you strike the outside by the stem, the impact will travel up the shell and break the casing.

Pet Toxicity: Hickory nuts are not toxic for your dog, but your pup's digestive system cannot digest them properly, so they could cause issues. Best to avoid them.

Black Cherry
Prunus serotina [PROO-nus seh-roh-TEE-nuh]

The Black Cherry is the largest wild cherry tree you'll find. It is a part of the *Rosaceae* (rose) family and goes by several names, including wild cherry, black mountain cherry, and rum cherry tree, to name a few. The trees are often too tall for humans, but you can find some reachable cherries on low branches or smaller trees.

Black cherry trees grow best in shady areas with well-draining soil. They are in and around forests.

Identification:

GROWTH/SIZE: A *deciduous* tree that grows to a height of 60 to 80 feet.

BARK/STEM/ROOT: The bark of young trees is shiny and *lenticular*. The bark on mature trees develops a dark, scaly pattern. The inner bark tastes like bitter almonds.

LEAF: Dark green leaves measure 3-6 inches long by 3/4 - 1 1/2 inches wide. Alternate leaves have fine irregular teeth, an inconspicuous stem gland, and yellow-brown pubescence under the leaf. Yellow-orange hues dominate the fall foliage. It smells like bitter almonds when crushed.

Flower: From late April to May, multiple fragrant white 5-petaled flowers appear in pendulous racemes up to 6 inches long.

Fruit/Seed/Nut: Cherries are typically ready to harvest in August. Drooping clusters of 3/8-inch purple-black cherries ripen in late summer. The fruit has a bitter taste right off the tree.

Look-a-likes: Wild black cherries can be a safe choice for beginning foragers since they don't have any close look-a-likes, except chokeberries, which are also edible.

Caution: All parts of the plant are toxic except the fruits. If ingested, the substance can be fatal to humans and pets. Cyanide is incredibly toxic when plants are wilting and is found in the leaves, stems, and seeds. Symptoms of Cyanide poisoning may include gasping, weakness, excitement, dilation of pupils, spasms, convulsions, coma, and respiratory failure.

Culinary Uses: You will have to remove the pits of the cherries before preparing them. You can freeze, dry, or process them into jams, juices, or fruit rolls.

Medicinal Uses: The bark of black cherry trees has historically been used for treating tuberculosis, indigestion, bronchitis, and coughs. Infusions made from black cherry bark, made by boiling rather than steeping, were used to treat diarrhea and pain. The bark was also considered to have sedative and astringent properties. Various Native American tribes believed black cherry bark was effective for colds, fevers, chills, measles, thrush, laryngitis, worms, and burns. It was also used as a blood purifier.

Fun/Historical Fact: In ancient times and into the modern era, the cherry was associated with virginity. Some believe that the red-colored fruit with its enclosed seed represents the uterus. Traditionally, Danish women were expected to consume the first ripe fruit after the birth of their first child to ensure a prosperous harvest. Also, cherry wood is reddish-brown with a straight, tight grain, making it the premier wood for cabinetry making and flooring.

Pet Toxicity: All parts of these plants other than the fruit itself are considered toxic and contain cyanide.

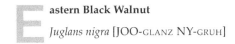

E **astern Black Walnut**

Juglans nigra [JOO-GLANZ NY-GRUH]

Black Walnuts are a delicacy, which means they're a fantastic find for foragers. They are native to the United States and belong to the *Juglandaceae* (walnut) family. They are delicious and relatively easy to forage, although you need time to process them.

Black walnut trees grow in sunny areas, such as on the edges of forests, roadsides, or fields.

Identification:

GROWTH/SIZE: This native deciduous tree grows quickly and can reach heights of 75 feet.

BARK/STEM/ROOT: The stems range from black to brown and have V-shaped leaf scars with a bud inside. The mature bark is thick and brown. The rough diamond patterns on the bark are ridged and furrowed.

LEAF: In the spring, the leaves are 12 to 24 inches long, have 10 to 23 leaflets, ovate to lanceolate, and are finely serrated. It is common for leaves to fall sporadically during the season. In late spring, the leaves turn yellow-green; in the fall, they turn bright yellow.

135

FLOWER: During April and May, yellow-green, single-stemmed catkins appear in short spikes and are 2 1/2 to 5 1/2 inches long.

FRUIT/SEED/NUT: By October, the catkins become non-splitting, yellow-green husks that house an edible brown to black nut. These husks will begin to fall to the ground, which indicates they are ready for harvest. You can harvest earlier but must let the fruit ripen at home.

Look-a-likes: Many native trees, such as sumac, walnut, and hickory, have similar leaf structures, but all are edible.

Caution: Black walnuts have a terrible habit of releasing a black juice that stains everything. Wear gloves and clothes you don't care about when harvesting and processing these nuts.

Culinary Uses: Once the hulls are soft to the touch, they're ripe. Wear old clothes and use a small mallet to crack the nuts, peel off the hulls, and drop the walnuts into a big bucket of water. The walnuts are coated in black fluid and debris, so wash them thoroughly. Once they're clean, air dry, and don't let any critters nearby. Once completely dry, crack them with a heavy-duty nutcracker or nutpick and enjoy raw or roasted.

Medicinal Uses: As a supplement, black walnut is anti-parasitic and anti-fungal, helps increase digestive health, and helps to reduce excessive sweating.

Fun/Historical Fact: The early American settlers discovered black walnuts growing in mixed forests. The rich-brown heartwood is resistant to decay and is used in various building projects on the homestead where water or rain may be an issue, such as fence posts and windowsills. They also utilized the nuts from the trees as snacks while out in the fields, adding them to soups and stews or grinding them into a meal for baking. Because the nuts were so nutritious, they were collected and stored, unshelled, in the root cellars for the winter.

Pet Toxicity: Walnut trees are susceptible to mold after a rainy spell, which is considered to cause toxicity in dogs. Symptoms of walnut poisoning are heavy panting, restlessness, excess salivation, vomiting, muscle tremors, fever, seizures, liver damage, and even death if left untreated.

B utternut
Juglans cinerea [JOO-ɢʟᴀɴᴢ sɪɴ-ER-ee-ᴜʜ]

Butternuts are delicious. They taste similar to ordinary walnuts but without any bitter notes. The nut meat is creamy and mild. These trees are native to the United States, a part of the *Juglandaceae* (walnut) family, and are known as White walnuts, Lemon nuts, or Oil nuts. Sadly, the butternut trees are endangered, so finding one is rare.

Healthy butternut trees are tricky because of the dreaded butternut canker disease. Still, you can sometimes find them in the woods. They increase in sunny areas.

Identification:

Gʀᴏᴡᴛʜ/Sɪᴢᴇ: A native deciduous tree that grows at a medium rate. They make great shade trees as they grow up to 60 feet tall, and the tops spread just as wide.

Bᴀʀᴋ/Sᴛᴇᴍ/Rᴏᴏᴛ: The new stems are green or olive-brown with glandular and non-glandular hairs that become smooth with age. They are dense and downy, with a light brown color. The mature bark is smooth, grayish-brown, and contains scattered pale lenticels. A broad, shallow, dark gray to black furrow develops at the base of its narrow, flat-topped ridges. Diamond-shaped patterns can extend along the ridges.

137

LEAF: 10-20 inches long, compound, and grows in an alternate pattern. They have serrated margins and fine hairs on the upper and lower surfaces. The leaf shape is oblong to lanceolate, and they turn yellow in the fall.

FLOWER: Yellow-green male flowers with up to 15 stamens are found on slender, 2.5-5.5-inch-long catkins. Female flowers are tiny and appear as short terminal spikes at the ends of branches, measuring 1.5 to 2.5 inches in length. There are up to seven flowers on each spike. Sticky hairs cover the green ovary with a red stigma. April through June are the blooming months.

FRUIT/SEED/NUT: They are typically found in September and October. They have a distinctive football shape and a velvety, green husk that's slightly sticky.

Look-a-likes: Black walnut trees are almost identical to butternut trees, but the nuts look very different.

Caution: Contain a juice that stains and has a plant-killing chemical, so wear old clothes and dispose of the husks carefully. As with other nuts, discard any damaged or discolored nuts.

Culinary Uses: Use a mallet for popping off the husks. If there's resistance, let the nuts rest until the husks go yellow. Dry the husks for a few weeks, then use a nutcracker to crack and enjoy. Dried nuts should store well.

Medicinal Uses: In North American Indigenous cultures, butternut was used as a laxative and tonic for rheumatism, arthritis, headaches, dysentery, constipation, and wounds.

Fun/Historical Fact: During the Civil War, the term "butternut" was sometimes applied to Confederate soldiers. Some of their uniforms faded from gray to tan or light brown. It's possible that butternut was used to color several Confederate soldiers' uniforms. The resemblance of these uniforms to butternut-dyed clothing resulted in the nickname.

Pet Toxicity: As this is a walnut tree, the nuts are susceptible to the same mold as the Eastern Black Walnut and, therefore, toxic to your pup. All of the same symptoms of poisoning apply to this tree as well.

Chinese Chestnut

Castanea mollissima [KAS-TAY-nee-uh MAW-LISS-ih-MUH]

Originating in China, Taiwan, and Korea, the Chinese Chestnut was introduced in the United States in the 1890s. It's a part of the **Fagaceae** (beech) family. Its sole purpose was to be used in orchards to enlarge harvests due to its smaller, more compact size than the American chestnut.

Chestnut trees are commonly found in wooded areas, but you can sometimes find a single one in fields or parks.

Identify:

GROWTH/SIZE: A deciduous rapidly growing tree that ranges in size between 40-60 feet. Branches usually grow low, making it easier to harvest.

BARK/STEM/ROOT: An adult plant has ridged or plated bark and ranges from green to brown to gray.

LEAF: The leaves are dark green and 5 to 8 inches long, oblong-lanceolate, coarsely toothed, soft green, and pubescent underneath. Fall brings yellow hues to the leaves.

FLOWER: The fragrant flower appears in catkins in late spring or early summer.

There are male and female flowers on the catkin, with the male flowers at the top and the female flowers at the base. Even short-lived flowers can be quite showy.

FRUIT/SEED/NUT: Chestnuts are crisp, meaty, and sweet but aren't as sweet as American chestnuts. The oval, round nuts measure 1 and 3 inches long and ripen between mid-September and October. Chestnuts are encased in spiny, dehiscent burs 2 to 3 inches round, usually containing two to three nuts each.

Look-a-likes: Horse chestnuts are toxic. The best way to tell the difference is by looking at the burrs. Edible chestnut burrs have a lot of spines very close together. Horse chestnut burrs have sparse spines, and the nut inside has no hairy tufts.

Caution: Some people can find the smell of flowers offensive for a short period. Soft, spiny nuts can be hazardous on sidewalks and while harvesting.

Culinary Uses: Hopefully, the spiny burrs will break when the nut falls from the tree. Otherwise, carefully crush them to remove the smooth, shiny nuts. Cut a small 'X' in the hull of each chestnut. These nuts have two, a rigid outer hull and a papery inner hull. You can soak them in hot water, hull them before roasting, or leave them on while roasting.

Medicinal Uses: The stem bark soothes infected wounds. The hulls are rich in tannin and are astringent. A decoction effectively treats diarrhea, uncontrollable bleeding, dysentery, regurgitation, and dehydration. Flowers are beneficial in treating tuberculosis.

Fun/Historical Fact: Sadly, the Chinese chestnut carried a blight that ravaged the American chestnut to near extinction. The Chinese version of the tree naturally resisted the blight, so it was virtually unphased. Since then, a cross-breeding program has been initiated to help save the American chestnut. Though it is still possible to find the native American variety, the Chinese chestnuts are delicious enough for hopeful foragers.

Pet Toxicity: non-toxic to your pup.

Shagbark Hickory

Carya ovata [KAIR-ʏᴜʜ ᴏʜ-VAY-ᴛᴜʜ]

Hickory nuts taste like pecans and walnuts and are great to enjoy raw. The Shagbark is a part of the *Juglandaceae* (walnut) family. They're easy to find, and the flavor of wild, foraged nuts is much better than what you can get in the store. Hickory nuts are relatively easy to process as well.

Shagbark hickory trees grow in deciduous forests.

Identification:

Gʀᴏᴡᴛʜ/Sɪᴢᴇ: This large, deciduous tree grows well over 100 feet tall and can live for over 350 years.

Bᴀʀᴋ/Sᴛᴇᴍ/Rᴏᴏᴛ: A bright white lenticule is scattered evenly over the surface of stout, light gray, light brown, or reddish-brown twigs. It becomes shaggy as it ages, as thin, flat plates develop one to three feet long, separate from the trunk, and curve away.

Lᴇᴀꜰ: It has compound leaves 8-14 inches long, alternate, yellow-green, and oddly pinnate. Leaflets are broad-lance-shaped, pointed, and finely toothed. The leaflets can range in length from 3-7 inches and width from 1-3 inches, with the terminal leaflet being the largest. The undersides are pale green and may have a few hairs along the veins. In the fall, the leaves turn yellow to a golden brown.

141

FLOWER: May is when this monoecious plant produces its non-showy, greenish-yellow flowers. 3-5 inch pendulous catkins form the male flowers, and short spikes form the female flowers.

FRUIT/SEED/NUT: Fruit size is 1 1/2-2 inches long by 2 inches wide. It is green when young but turns dark brown and splits open when mature. The nuts of each fruit are light tan, oval, and somewhat compressed. Hickory nuts can be harvested from the ground in the fall, typically during November.

Look-a-likes: none known

Caution: Like other nuts, bugs and critters alike will compete with you. Be prepared to throw out any nuts with holes, discoloration, or mold.

Culinary Uses: Throw the rest into a large pot of water after removing any suspect nuts. Nuts that sink are best, and the floaters might have been eaten or shriveled up. Crack the floaters right away and save the sinkers. Some are still good to eat, but get rid of others. You can eat hickory nuts raw or toast them to improve the flavor.

Medicinal Uses: Small shoots were steamed and used as an inhalant to treat headaches. A decoction has been taken internally or applied as a poultice to joints to help with rheumatism.

Fun/Historical Fact: The Shagbark nuts can be used as a substitute for the pecan. The tree's bark can be used to make maple syrup. Native Americans used Shagbark wood to smoke their meat after a successful hunt and to produce the bows they hunted with. Shagbark hickory, like its cousins, has been used to make all types of tools and tool handles due to the wood's strength.

Pet Toxicity: Hickory nuts are not toxic for your dog, but your pup's digestive system cannot digest them properly, so they could cause issues. Best to avoid them.

White Oak
Quercus alba [KWER-kus AL-ba]

Almost everyone knows that whiskey is aged in charred new oak barrels, but did you know that barrels made of American white oak are also used for aging wine? It's a part of the *Fagaceae* (walnut) family. It has several other names, Forked-leaf White Oak, Northern White Oak, and Quebec Oak, are just a few. The name is derived from the color of the finished wood.

It's usually found in forested areas of dry slopes, valleys, and ravines. You may find single trees in parks, fields, and meadows.

Identification:

GROWTH/SIZE: North America's eastern and central parts are home to this species. The oldest specimens have been documented to be over 450 years old. A mature tree typically reaches an elevation of 80–100 feet. The lower branches of this tree tend to extend far out laterally, parallel to the ground, leading to a massive canopy.

BARK/STEM/ROOT: Smooth, light gray bark covers the branches. There are scattered white lenticels on the twigs, which are reddish-brown to purplish-brown. Generally, the bark is white or grayish and scaly. Furrows are shallow and divided into vertical blocks or flat, narrow plates. Over time, they will become flaky.

Leaf: Each leaf has five to nine deep, rounded, and even lobes and is 4 to 9 inches long and 2 to 4 inches wide. Their tip is rounded, and their base is wedge-shaped. Alternate, simple, elliptic, oblong, oblong-obovate, and cuneate leaves are found on this plant. Green in color, with a whitish or glaucous underside. It develops late in autumn and is purplish brown to reddish brown. A few leaves may persist into winter.

Flower: Blooming in April, the male flower is arranged in clusters of greenish-yellow catkins in long pendulous chains about 2 - 3 1/2 inches long. A female flower is not as showy and appears as a few greenish-red spots in the axils of emerging leaves.

Fruit/Seed/Nut: September through November is the time when the nuts appear. Initially green, they ripen to a light brown color. Fruits are 3/4 to 1-inch elongated acorns with shallow cups that cover 1/4 to 1/3 of the nut. Acorns mature in their first year and can be numerous.

Look-a-likes: none known

Caution: Look out for damaged acorns with holes or discoloration.

Culinary Uses: First, put them in water and discard any floating to the top. Then, dry the acorns. Once they're dry, crack open the shells and grind or mash them. Finally, leach out the tannins in the acorns by soaking the mash in water. Leaching can take hours or weeks, and you may need to switch out the water periodically.

Medicinal Uses: In addition to its antiseptic and astringent properties, it is also an expectorant and tonic. Boiling the bark and drinking the liquid helps ease bleeding, diarrhea, fevers, coughs and colds, and asthma. Chewing the bark has helped to treat mouth ulcers. On the skin, it can be used as a wash to soothe burns, rashes, bruises, ulcers, etc., and on the vaginal area as a douche. Muscle pains have also been treated with it.

Fun/Historical Fact: The Japanese use white oak extensively for their martial arts weapons.

Pet Toxicity: Oak leaves and nuts contain gallic and tannic acids, which can harm pets. If eaten, symptoms are usually mild, including stomach discomfort, vomiting, and diarrhea.

PART SIX
MUSHROOM AND FUNGI

MUSHROOM WARNING PLEASE READ:

Mushroom foraging can be fun and rewarding. Still, it is crucial to be cautious and correctly identify mushrooms before consuming them. Many wild mushrooms are poisonous and can cause severe illness or even death if ingested.

Learning how to correctly identify mushrooms by consulting field guides, attending foraging classes, or going out with experienced foragers is essential. Some key characteristics to look for include the cap, stem, and gills' shape, color, and texture. It's also important to take note of the mushroom's habitat and the plants and trees it is growing near.

When foraging, avoid mushrooms with white gills; they are often toxic. Also, it's necessary to avoid mushrooms with red color on the cap or stem since many poisonous mushrooms have red pigmentation.

It's also important to never eat raw mushrooms because some toxic mushrooms can cause severe reactions.

It's also important to note that some mushrooms may be edible but cause allergic reactions in specific individuals. Hence, it is vital to start with small portions when trying a new mushroom species.

It is always best to err on the side of caution and only consume mushrooms that an expert has positively identified.

66 SAFEST WAY TO COOK MUSHROOMS

MUSHROOM WARNING, PLEASE READ:

Mushroom foraging can be fun and rewarding. Still, it is crucial to be cautious and correctly identify mushrooms before consuming them. Many wild mushrooms are poisonous and can cause severe illness or even death if ingested.

Learning how to correctly identify mushrooms by consulting field guides, attending foraging classes, or going out with experienced foragers is essential. Some key characteristics to look for include the cap, stem, and gills' shape, color, and texture. It's also important to take note of the mushroom's habitat and the plants and trees it is growing near.

When foraging, avoid mushrooms with white gills; they are often toxic. Also, it's necessary to avoid mushrooms with red color on the cap or stem since many poisonous mushrooms have red pigmentation.

It's also important to never eat raw mushrooms because some toxic mushrooms can cause severe reactions.

It's also important to note that some mushrooms may be edible but cause allergic reactions in specific individuals. Hence, it is vital to start with small portions when trying a new mushroom species.

It is always best to err on the side of caution and only consume mushrooms that an expert has positively identified.

Cleaning and Cooking Mushrooms

Cooking mushrooms enhances their taste and helps break down their cell walls, making nutrients more accessible and reducing potentially harmful compounds. To ensure you're cooking mushrooms safely and deliciously, follow these tactics, temps, and cooking methods.

1. **Clean mushrooms gently:** Use a damp paper towel or a soft brush to remove dirt and debris. Avoid soaking them in water, as they can become waterlogged and lose their texture.
2. **Choose the proper cooking method:** There are various ways to cook mushrooms, including sautéing, roasting, grilling, and stir-frying. Sautéing is a popular method that involves cooking mushrooms in a bit of oil or butter over medium heat, which helps to release their natural moisture and develop a rich flavor. Roasting and grilling mushrooms at a high temperature can create a crispy, golden exterior with a tender interior. Stir-frying is another quick and easy way to cook mushrooms while retaining their texture.
3. **Cook at a safe temperature:** To eliminate potentially harmful compounds, cook mushrooms at a minimum temperature of 165°F (74°C). Use a food thermometer to ensure they reach this internal temperature.
4. **Cook until tender and golden:** The ideal texture for cooked mushrooms is tender and slightly golden. This usually takes around 8-10 minutes for sautéing, 15-20 minutes for roasting, and 5-7 minutes for stir-frying. Cooking times may vary depending on the type and size of the mushrooms.
5. **Season to taste:** Enhance the flavor of your mushrooms by seasoning them with salt, pepper, garlic, onions, or your favorite herbs and spices. Add seasonings towards the end of the cooking process to prevent them from burning.

Following these guidelines, you can safely cook mushrooms to unlock their full flavor potential and nutritional benefits while reducing any risks of consuming them raw.

E ntoloma

Entoloma abortivum [EN-TO-LOH-MA AB-OR-TI-VUM]

There are aborted and non-aborted versions of this mushroom. The aborted version of the mushrooms looks a bit like popcorn. They are a part of the **Entolomataceae** family. These mushrooms result from a parasitic reaction between two species of mushroom, honey mushrooms and Entolomas, that creates this distinctive and delicious deformed mushroom. The common name for this mushroom is Shrimp of the Woods.

They can be found near tree roots and dead wood, so look in woodlands. You can also find them in the fields. They appear primarily in mid-September through October, when Armillaria (honey) starts to grow heavily.

Identification:

CAP: It is initially convex with an in-rolled margin but later becomes flat.

GILLS: Grayish at first; the gills turn pink with age and run down the stalk slightly. Fruit that has been aborted does not have gills.

STEM: Usually, the stipe measures 1-4 inches long and 1/4 - 1/2 inches thick, with the length corresponding roughly to the cap width. There is often a slight enlargement of the base. The aborted version often has no stem, and its interior is usually brown, striated, or pithy.

FLESH: In the gilled version, it is white, reasonably dense, and meaty. In contrast, the aborted version is pithy inside and has a pinkish tone. The gills may bruise slightly pink. It may be possible to find air space. When cracks in the cap have allowed water, dirt, or bugs to enter, older ones can develop brown rot spots. Due to their ability to absorb water, they must be cleaned carefully.

SPORE: Non-aborted gilled fruits are pink to rouge.

ODOR/TASTE: The texture is similar to shrimp, but it has a mild mushroom flavor.

Look-a-likes: There are no lookalikes to the aborted form, and it is entirely safe for harvesting.

Caution: The non-aborted version strongly resembles toxic mushrooms and should not be harvested without an expert guiding the way.

Culinary Uses: Brush clean in the field and give them an extra clean at home. These mushrooms are best fried and caramelized. Because of their texture, you can use them as you would shrimp. You can also slice them and dehydrate them.

Medicinal Uses: none known

Black Chanterelle

Craterellus cornucopioides [CRA-TER-EL-LUS COR-NU-CO-PI-OI-DES]

Black chanterelles are sometimes known as Horn of Plenty or Black Trumpets. They have a delicate, smoky flavor, making them a fantastic treat for foragers. They're related to the more prized chanterelles, but while they're harder to spot, it's well worth the effort.

These remarkable fungi prefer damp and shaded environments, where they flourish amidst the forest floor.

Identification:

CAP: This fruiting body is not separated into stalk and cap. It resembles a funnel with the opening expanded at the top. It can grow to a height of 4 inches and a diameter of 1/4-2 3/4 inches but has been reported to reach a maximum height of 6 inches on occasion.

HYMENIUM: A unique hymenium that consists of irregularly spaced ridges and folds rather than the typical gills or pores found in many other mushroom species. These ridges are highly distinctive and make black chanterelles easily recognizable. The hymenium of black chanterelles is usually a dark gray to black color, which is one of the key features.

151

STIPE: The stipe is typically black or very dark brown. The color is uniform throughout the stem. It has a slightly fragile and hollow structure, making it less substantial than the caps. Depending on the mushroom size, it may be only a few inches long. The stipe is attached centrally to the cap's underside, extending downward into the ground. The attachment is typically smooth and not flaring.

SPORE PRINT: dark brown to black in color

ECOLOGY: Black chanterelles are known to thrive during the late summer, fall, or early winter, depending on the specific region and climate. Black chanterelles establish a mutually beneficial relationship by forming mycorrhizal associations with trees. The fungus assists the host tree in absorbing essential nutrients like phosphorus and water, while the tree provides carbohydrates through photosynthesis. This partnership benefits the mushroom and the tree and plays a crucial role in maintaining the health and growth of forest ecosystems. Black chanterelles contribute to nutrient absorption, water retention, soil structure, and the decomposition of organic matter.

Look-a-likes: The mushroom has no poisonous look-a-likes, making it a great mushroom for beginners to identify.

Caution: none known

Culinary Uses: Rinse well before cooking. Sauté. It works particularly well with creamy sauces. You can harvest trumpet mushrooms two ways: pull them from the ground, cut off the end and any dirt, then place them in a basket, or you can use scissors to cut the mushrooms at the base, leaving the dirty bottoms behind, and keeping your mushrooms clean.

Medicinal Uses: The black trumpet has a considerable amount of vitamin B-12. As well as being vital to the formation of red blood cells, vitamin B-12 is also essential to the metabolic function of cells and the functioning of nerves. Vitamin B-12 deficiency can cause fatigue, mood problems, anemia, muscle weakness, intestinal problems, and nerve damage. Dementia and low cognitive function may also result from it, as well as heart and blood vessel disease.

B lewit
Clitocybe nuda [CLI-TO-CY-BE NU-DA]

Otherwise known as a Blue cap, Blue hat, and Blue leg, Wood Blewit has a strong flavor, making it a fantastic ingredient for cooking. It's also known to have potential medicinal properties, such as possible anti-diabetic and anti-hyperglycemic effects.

A deciduous and mixed woodland species, often fruiting well into December when temperatures are mild. It grows in leaf litter and can be found during autumn and winter.

Identification:

Cap: A young specimen with a convex cap with an in-rolled margin will be lighter. A mature sample will have a flat cap with an uplifted, wavy margin measuring from 1 5/8 to 5 7/8 inches across and will be darker.

Hymenium: These are attached to the stem, sometimes by a notch, are densely packed, have short gills, and are pale lavender or lilac in color when young, fading to buff or pinkish-buff with age.

Stipe: Gills are attached to the short, stout stem, which is about 3 1/4-2 3/8 inches long, sometimes larger.

FLESH: A blewit's color varies depending on age. In younger mushrooms, it can be lilac, purplish, or deep purple; as it ages, it will change to cream-colored or almost brown.

SPORE: Spore prints of wood blewits are white to pale pink, which makes them easy to identify.

ODOR/TASTE: Blewits have a distinctive odor, often compared to the smell of frozen orange juice.

Look-a-likes: It has a few look-a-likes; some are edible, like the Sordid blewit (*Lepista sordida*). The Amethyst deceiver (*Laccaria amethystina*) can be confused with blewit, but it is also edible.

Caution: The clouded agaric and purple Cortinarius mushrooms are toxic, however. The cloudier agaric mushroom has a grey-brown cap and creamy gills that continue down the stem. In contrast, the purple Cortinarius mushrooms have sturdy stems with a web-like coating.

Culinary Uses: Blewits should never be eaten raw; they must be cooked thoroughly. The most enjoyable flavors are those that are subtle. Getting overly creative will result in tasting a mushroom's texture with no flavor. Like other mushrooms, they're delicious in a cream sauce, but I prefer them simply cooked. For the most delicious results, cook mushrooms and buttons young or in large pieces to preserve their texture.

Medicinal Uses: Blewit is primarily beneficial nutritionally, but some believe it may also have medicinal potential. It is traditionally used in wound care and thiamine deficiency prevention.

C hanterelles

Genus cantharellus [CAN-THA-REL-LUS]

Chanterelles come in many colors: red, golden, and yellowfoot, to name just a few. Chanterelles are one of the ultimate wild mushrooms because they must be foraged rather than cultivated. Thankfully, they're easy to spot and delicious, with a peppery, earthy flavor.

A chanterelle can be associated with conifers or hardwood trees depending on its species. It is common to find them in forests with oaks, silver birches, Western hemlock trees, and Scots pine, especially when the undergrowth is moist and mossy. They are usually found in the same places as wild blueberries, but this is not guaranteed. A walk through the woods following rain should be fruitful from late July through September.

Identification:

CAP: This fruiting body is not separated into stalk and cap. It resembles a funnel with the opening expanded at the top. It can grow to a height of 4 inches and a diameter of 1/4-2 3/4 inches but has been reported to reach a maximum height of 6 inches on occasion.

FLESH: Aside from the Black trumpet we've discussed in a previous chapter, this genus has several species. They all have the same type of flesh but come in many colors ranging from whiteish yellow to orange.

SPORE: cream to buff

ODOR/TASTE: fragrant and fruity

Look-a-likes: The most common look-alike is the Jack-o-Lantern (*Omphalotus olearius*), which is the same color as the golden chanterelle. However, it has true gills. Chanterelles smell sweet and nutty when you pick them, but Jack-o-Lanterns don't.

Caution: none known

Prepare Clean well and store chanterelles in the refrigerator. Chanterelles work well in a lot of dishes or when fried in butter. You can also preserve them by drying them and turning them into a flavor-boosting powder. Generally, Chanterelles match well with eggs, curry, chicken, pork, fish, beef, and veal. They can be topped on pizzas, stewed, marinated, sautéed, or used as a filling for crêpes.

As you can see, Chanterelles can be added to many different dishes. It is common for mushroom enthusiasts to sauté chanterelles in butter with a pinch of salt, a clove of freshly crushed garlic, and a small amount of whipping cream. This recipe emphasizes the chanterelle flavor without being overpowered by other aromas. The recipe keeps its flavor after being frozen, which makes it an excellent option for lunches and dinners.

Medicinal Uses: Many species of chanterelles contain antioxidant carotenoids. Vitamin D is also abundant in them.

Chicken of the Woods

laetiporus sulphureus [LAE-TI-POR-US SUL-PHU-REUS]

Chicken of the woods is a distinctive species of bracket fungus. It has several other names, such as crab-of-the-woods, sulfur polypore, and sulfur shelf. It is not uncommon for a dead log or tree to yield ten, twenty, thirty, or more pounds.

You can find Chicken of the Woods in hardwood forests. Look for fallen, rotting hardwood trees from May to November.

Identification:

Gills: It has tubelike pores rather than gills on the underside of the fruit body.

Stem: lacks a stipe

Flesh: Initially knob-shaped, the fruiting body expands into fan-shaped shelves, growing in overlapping layers directly from the tree trunk. It has a suede-like texture and is sulfur-yellow to bright orange. Shelf widths may range from 2 to 23 1/2 inches, and thicknesses up to 1 1/2 inches. It is common for the fruit bodies to turn tan or white after they have matured.

Spore: white

Odor/Taste: When you get close, it may have a sulfurous smell.

157

Look-a-likes: *Laetiporus huroniensis* - Their characteristics are shared with L. sulphureus, including a yellow to orange colored cap and pale undersides. Additionally, they have yellow pores and grow on bracket shelves. There is only one main difference between these fungi and other Laetiporus species: they thrive on hemlock trees, a highly poisonous flowering tree.

Laetiporus gilbertsonii shares most characteristics with L. Sulphureus but is found growing on conifer trees. This fungus is edible but may cause gastrointestinal issues.

Caution: This mushroom may cause gastrointestinal upset in some people, so raw consumption is not recommended. Test it in small servings first to avoid this.

Culinary Uses: Freshly picked, the flesh is succulent with a pleasant fungal smell and exudes a yellowish, transparent juice but soon becomes dry and crumbly. Chicken of the woods has a meaty texture and can be grilled or fried like chicken or tofu. It is advisable to store mushrooms in containers that allow some gas exchange rather than containers that don't. Therefore, storing mushrooms in paper bags rather than plastic bags is better. Mushrooms should not be kept in an airtight bag.

Medicinal Uses: In folk medicine, it treats coughs, pyretic diseases, gastric cancer, and rheumatism.

G iant Puffball
calvatia gigantea [CAL-VA-SHIA GI-GAN-TIA]

Puffballs are delightfully named mushrooms that are equally delightful to forage. Like all mushrooms, never harvest any mushroom you're unfamiliar with. Thankfully, puffball mushrooms are easy to spot and common.

Typically found in meadows, fields, and deciduous forests in the late summer and autumn.

Identification:

CAP: has no discernible cap.

GILLS: has no discernible gills.

STEM: has no discernible stem.

FLESH: The average puffball grows 4 - 20 inches in diameter. The inside of mature giant puffballs is greenish brown, whereas the interior of immature puffballs is white.

SPORE: Unlike most mushrooms, giant puffballs produce all their spores inside the fruiting body; a large specimen may contain several trillion spores. There is a yellowish color to the spores; they are smooth and 3 to 5 μm in size. The spore print is brown.

ODOR/TASTE: A uniform white color must be present in the interior tissue. Whenever it is yellowish or brown, it means it is approaching maturity and could be toxic or off-flavoring.

Look-a-likes: Some mushrooms, such as *Scleroderma* species, are mildly poisonous, small, thick-skinned, and collectively known as false puffballs. Even at a young age, false puffballs are usually dark to dark purple inside, with tough, thick skin.

Caution: If the inside isn't solid or discolored, throw it out. It's either an inedible earth ball or further along its growth cycle, but either way, it's not safe to eat.

Culinary Uses: Store in the refrigerator and brush clean before use. You can use it as you would any other mushroom or even use it as a replacement for an eggplant.

Medicinal Uses: The giant puffball served as a styptic dressing to stop bleeding from wounds.

H en of the Woods

grifola frondosa [GRI-FO-LA FRON-DOSA]

Despite what you might think, Hen of the Woods differs from Chicken of the Woods. It's known as maitake and can grow to a considerable size. Other common names are ram's head or sheep's head.

Hen of the Woods is a parasitic mushroom that grows on trees. Typically, they prefer oak trees. You can find them in oak forests or where a few oaks grow.

Identification: These are shelf mushrooms. They're usually grayish brown, which makes them hard to spot. Hen of the woods looks a bit like coral growing on the base of a tree, with folds that develop out from a solid core. The flesh is white.

CAP: Often curled or spoon-shaped, with wavy margins, the caps are 1–4 inches wide.

GILLS: Every cap has between one and three pores per millimeter, with tubes rarely exceeding 1/8 inch deep.

STEM: As the mushroom matures, its milky-white stipe becomes tough and branchy.

FLESH: It develops from a potato-sized underground structure known as a sclerotium. The fruiting body usually grows to 40 inches, but can be as long as 60 inches. The cluster consists of grayish-brown caps.

Spore: There are white pores that are decurrent. Young pores are round and small, but as they age, they become angular and larger. There is a white spore print.

Odor/Taste: They have a mild and pleasant flavor.

Look-a-likes: A few look-a-likes are primarily edible, if not always as palatable. Always check for bugs and worms.

Caution: Older Hen of the Woods are very difficult to clean, as debris can work its way into the flesh of the mushrooms. Take care when cleaning and ideally pick them young.

Culinary Uses: Separate into clusters and trim the dirt off the bottom. If necessary, remove any debris and cut it into slices to check for hidden surprises. You can pickle, dehydrate, or cook and freeze them for later use. Otherwise, cook as you would any other meaty mushroom. You can even make steaks.

Medicinal Uses: As a result of its ability to stimulate the immune system, it helps the body fight various types of cancer. Moreover, this mushroom has been shown to have hypoglycemic properties and may benefit diabetics.

Honey
armillaria mellea [AR-MIL-LA-RIA MIL-LEA]

Commonly known by several names, such as stump mushroom, stumpie, pipinky, or pinky. These mushrooms are formed when the tree develops Armillaria root rot; this disease will kill the tree. Honey mushrooms tend to grow in huge swathes, so if you find one, the chances are that you'll find loads more.

Commonly found in clusters, but sometimes singly on wood or buried wood, mostly hardwoods. They appear soon after the first fall rains with continued fruiting through mid-winter.

Identification:

CAP: The cap is smooth and measures one and six inches in diameter. At first, it is convex but flattens with age, often with a central raised umbo, then becomes somewhat dish-shaped. A mature cap usually has arched margins and is sticky when wet.

GILLS: Initially white, they may turn pinkish-yellow or discolored as they age. They are broad, distant, and attached to the stipe at right angles or slightly decurrent.

STEM: The stipe can reach as much as 8 inches long and has a diameter of 1 1/2 inches. At first, it has a fibrillose texture and a spongy consistency but later becomes hollow. The stipes are fused to the stipes of other mushrooms in a clump

163

at its base, which is cylindrical. The upper end is white, and the lower is brownish-yellow, often with a dark base. The upper part of the stipe is covered with a persistent and skin-like ring. When young, a white partial veil protects the gills and has a velvety margin with yellowish fluff underneath.

FLESH: Despite its typical honey color, this fungus can sometimes have dark, hairy scales near the center arranged radially.

SPORE: White

ODOR/TASTE: The taste has been described as slightly sweet and nutty, with a chewy to crunchy texture, depending on how it is prepared.

Look-a-likes: There are a few toxic look-a-likes, including the deadly Galerina, Pholiota mushrooms, and sulfur tufts. You can identify it because it has a bell-shaped cap. If you aren't sure, don't risk it.

Caution: digestive concerns have been reported

Culinary Uses: You should always thoroughly cook honey mushrooms. Prepare these mushrooms as you would any other. The bitter taste in some mushrooms can be removed by parboiling them before consumption, which may reduce the number of gastrointestinal irritations. It is recommended that they be cooked before eating. Although reconstituted mushrooms are tough to swallow, drying them preserves and intensifies their flavor. It is also possible to pickle and roast these mushrooms.

Medicinal Uses: none known

Fun/Historical Fact: Some honey mushrooms possess a bioluminescent ability; the mycelium glows in the dark, but not the fruiting bodies, producing a green light.

King Bolete

boletus edulis [BO-LE-TUS ED-U-LIS]

Bolete mushrooms are known as the King of Mushrooms for a good reason. They belong to the **Boletaceae** family, and other familiar names include penny bun, porcino, or porcini.

Porcini mushrooms are most commonly found along the fringes of woodlands. They especially like conifers and oak trees.

Identification:

CAP: A mature plant reaches a width of 3-12 inches. The mushroom's shape is convex when young, flattens as it ages, and has a slightly sticky feel to the touch. Generally, it has a reddish-brown color that fades to white near the margin, and as it matures, it darkens more.

GILLS/PORES: Tiny and angular pores do not stain when bruised. Pores are roughly two to three per millimeter. The pores appear white and filled with cotton (mycelia) when they are young; with age, they turn yellow, then brown.

STIPE/STEM: The stipe is tall and thick, ranging from 3 to 10 inches, which is large compared to caps. Often, it bulges out in the middle or has a club shape. The upper portion is finely reticulate, while the lower is smooth or irregularly ridged.

FLESH: Young fruit bodies have white, thick, firm flesh, but the flesh becomes softer with age. Bruised or cut plants either do not change or change to a very light brown or light red color.

SPORE: Olive Brown

ODOR/TASTE: The taste is nutty and slightly meaty, with a smooth, creamy texture and a distinctive smell of sourdough.

Look-a-likes: A similar-looking plant is the Devil's bolete (Rubroboletus satanas), which bears a red stem and bruises blue. Another lookalike is the Bitter Bolete, which isn't poisonous but has an incredibly bitter taste.

Caution: Toxic boletes look normal but have reddish parts. Other toxic look-a-likes will turn blue or black when cut.

Culinary Uses: Significant fruiting occurs after the first soaking rains of autumn, with sporadic fruiting occurring during the spring and summer. Porcini mushrooms go wonderfully in any wild dish because of their excellent flavor, such as risotto. You can also dry them or freeze them to preserve them. If frozen for longer than four months, the color, smell, and taste of porcini significantly diminish.

Medicinal Uses: King boletes have been used as antioxidants, as potential anti-cancer growth inhibitors, to relieve constipation, to protect the liver from damage, and as an antimicrobial.

Fun/Historical Fact: Around the world, King Bolete is considered the most prized wild mushroom. It's the safest wild edible mushroom for beginners.

L obster

hypomyces lactifluorum [HY-PO-MY-CES LAC-TI-FLOR-UM]

Lobster mushrooms are named such because they taste and smell like seafood, specifically lobsters. They're easy to identify because they look so bizarre. They are parasitic fungi, attacking other fungi and changing them drastically.

A lobster mushroom usually appears in deciduous woods with oaks and poplars in midsummer to early fall. They are often found near small ponds, clearings, and campsites in the forest.

Identification: Despite its common name, this is not a mushroom. Instead, it is a parasitic fungus that grows on mushrooms, making it a reddish-orange color similar to a lobster's shell. Lactarius, Lactifluus (milk caps), and Russula (brittle gills) are specifically affected.

FLESH: A hard, orange covering that attacks rapidly and quickly engulfs the host. The surface is dotted with tiny pimples.

ODOR/TASTE: They have a seafood-like flavor and a firm, dense texture.

Look-a-likes: As with any mushroom, approach cautiously and eat a small portion first.

Caution: Discard any with white mold.

Culinary Uses: Clean any dirt and cook lightly with delicate flavors. Overcooking can interfere with the unique seafood flavor and texture. In excess, dried lobsters can become bitter. However, lobster mushrooms love contact with heat and fat. It is possible to curb any bitterness and deepen their flavor by exposing them to heat and fat, whether fresh or dried. A saffron/turmeric effect occurs when lobster mushrooms are exposed to fat and heat. A delicious risotto can be made with this, or compound butter can be made with this. Mix lobster mushrooms with other mushrooms to add a touch of variety to your cooking.

Medicinal Uses: Though considered healthy, lobster is not well-known as a medicinal mushroom.

Oyster

pleurotus ostreatus [PLU-RO-TUS OS-TRE-TUS]

Oyster mushrooms are very good for you and grow in abundance. They have a delicious, meaty taste. Common names for this mushroom include oyster fungus, hiratake, or pearl oyster mushroom. The oyster mushroom is one of the few carnivorous mushrooms known. The mushroom's mycelia kill and digest nematodes which produce nitrogen.

Oyster mushrooms grow on dead, deciduous trees. You can find oyster mushrooms in the fall. The oyster mushroom is best picked when young; as it ages, the flesh becomes tough, and the flavor becomes acrid.

Identification:

CAP: It has a broad, fan, or oyster-shaped cap ranging from 3/4 to 11 3/4 inches. Specimens are white, gray, tan, or dark brown, with smooth margins and often an in-rolled or wavy margin as young specimens.

GILLS: It has white to cream gills that descend on the stalk if it has one.

STEM: Often, the mushroom's stipe does not exist. Whenever it is present, it is short and thick, off-centered, and attached laterally to the wood.

FLESH: It is white, firm, and varies in thickness because of the arrangement of the stipes.

SPORE: Viewing the mushroom spore print on a dark background is recommended since it is white to lilac-gray.

ODOR/TASTE: An anise-like flavor and a bittersweet almond aroma describe the flavor of the mushroom.

Look-a-likes: This mushroom is similar to the Angel Wing mushroom, which is edible for many people (though some people have issues). Angel Wings grow on conifers and are pure white and more delicate than oyster mushrooms.

Caution: While toxic Lentinellus species can look similar, they are distinguished by their jagged gills and finely-haired caps.

Culinary Uses: You can keep them in the refrigerator for a few days, freeze them, or dehydrate them. The oysters must be cooked before eating and are lovely when fried with salt and pepper.

Medicinal Uses: Antioxidants in oyster mushrooms help prevent cellular damage. They may also reduce heart disease risk factors like high blood pressure and cholesterol and regulate blood sugar levels.

Shaggy Mane
coprinus comatus [Co-pri-nus co-ma-tus]

These mushrooms are easy to identify due to their distinctive shaggy cap, making them a fantastic option for beginners. They're also tasty and ordinary, which makes them an excellent choice for everyone else.

Summer and fall are the most suitable seasons to find them in grasses, wood chips, and hard-packed soil. They often grow just after rains that soak the ground. Groups may be scattered or arranged singly, but larger, tightly packed populations are more common.

Identification:

Cap: When the young fruit bodies emerge from the ground, they are white cylinders, then open to reveal bell-shaped caps. The fungus has white caps covered in scales, which gives it its common name. The shaggy ink cap is easily recognized by its almost cylindrical cap, which initially covers most of the stem. It ranges in width from 1 - 3 inches and height from 2 - 7 inches.

Gills: Below the cap, the gills start white, turn pink, and become black. They liquefy into a sludge-like liquid filled with spores (hence the name "ink cap") when they become black. A rapid change occurs in the free gills as they change from white to pink, then to black.

171

STEM: It is white and relatively thick, measures 2–16 inches high and 4 inches wide, and has a loose ring near the base.

FLESH: It is white, quite soft, and easy to break.

SPORE: black-brown

ODOR/TASTE: mild

Look-a-likes: Due to its similarity to shaggy mane and other edible mushrooms, the 'vomiter' mushroom (*Chlorophyllum molybdites*) is the most common cause of mushroom poisoning.

Caution: Similar to this plant is (*Coprinopsis atramentaria*) (the common ink cap), which contains coprine and can cause coprine poisoning when consumed with alcohol.

Culinary Uses: These mushrooms need to be cooked like other wild mushrooms. Prepare quickly, as the cap will rapidly go soggy and turn into ink, especially once bruised. You can use them as ordinary mushrooms, even once they've started to turn black. You can also use the link in your cooking, as it is edible and can color pasta dough or other food. You can also dehydrate shaggy mane mushrooms.

Medicinal Uses: Over fifty years ago, shaggy manes contained ergothioneine, a thiol compound with antioxidant properties. Antioxidant properties are closely related to anti-cancer, anti-inflammation, and anti-obesity properties. Several studies have demonstrated that consumption of *C. comatus* can help regulate blood glucose concentrations.

Fun/Historical Fact: This mushroom will turn black and dissolve within hours after being picked or spore-deposited.

White Button

agaricus bisporus [AG-A-RI-CUS BIS-SPOR-US]

The most common names for this mushroom are Portobello and Champignons, but it is also known as white, button, or table in its immature stage.

© Alan Rockefeller CC by 4.0

Best harvested from late spring to early fall. This mushroom can be found worldwide in grassy areas, typically after rain, and is commonly found in pastures around manure.

Identification:

CAP: Wild specimens have pale grey-brown caps with broad, flat scales on pale backgrounds that fade toward the margins. The fruit is at first hemispherical before it flattens out with maturity and measures between 2 and 4 inches in diameter.

GILLS: There are narrow, crowded gills that are pink at first, red-brown after that, and finally dark brown with a whitish edge.

STEM: It consists of a cylindrical stipe up to 2 1/2 inches tall and 1/2 - 3/4 inches wide, ringed on the upper side with thick and narrow streaks.

FLESH: While bruising stains it a pale pinkish-red, the meat is white.

SPORE: dark brown

Odor/Taste: mild and pleasant

Look-a-likes: There is a more common and less dangerous mistake of confusing Agaricus bisporus with Agaricus xanthodermus, an inedible mushroom that grows worldwide in grassy areas. Agaricus xanthodermus is scented like phenol; its flesh turns yellow when bruised. The fungus can cause nausea and vomiting in some people.

Caution: The common mushroom is often confused with young specimens of the deadly poisonous Destroying Angel (Amanita sp.). However, it can be distinguished from the latter by its volva or cup at the base and pure white gills.

Culinary Uses: Wash thoroughly. A whole mushroom will last longer than a cut one. Raw mushrooms can be stored in an open paper bag with a damp paper towel over the bag in the fridge. Though mushrooms do not do well when frozen, there are a few ways to prepare them, making freezing a viable option for later use. Sautéed mushrooms can be stored in the fridge or freezer and last up to a year if frozen. Steaming mushrooms will preserve their natural flavor and allow them to be held in the freezer for up to a year. Lastly, you can always dry your mushrooms in the oven or using a dehydrated.

Dehydrating is, in my opinion, the best way to store them if you are not going to use them immediately. This method allows for estimated 6-month storage. They maintain their fantastic flavor while taking up less space to store. The one thing to note is that moisture is the downfall of keeping any mushroom.

Medicinal Uses: In addition to being rich in nutrients such as carbohydrates, amino acids, fats, and minerals, this mushroom holds the potential to fight cancer, antioxidants, obesity, and inflammation.

White Morel

morchella americana [MOR-KEL-LA AMERICANA]

Morels are widely considered one of the best wild mushrooms that foragers can find. They are a native North American member of the **Morchellaceae** family. They're delicious and elusive enough that a fortunate forager typically keeps their morel spot close to their hearts.

Fruiting season is in spring for this species, mainly from March to June. They live in forests near more mature trees. Look around ash, elm, poplar, aspen, cottonwood, and apple trees for the best chance of finding them. Orchards are an excellent option. After forest fires, they thrive in logging areas, near streams, and loamy soil.

Identification:

CAP: Morchella americana has an egg-shaped head with a convex, bluntly conical, or almost round apex. There are pits and ridges in the head that are irregularly shaped, with broadly angled pits arranged either randomly or vertically. There is a yellow-to-brown coloration to the cap overall. It is worth noting that the depth and color of the cap's ridges and pits differ depending on the age of the mushroom. The cap is attached directly to the stalk without a significant overhang or rim. The average height of the cap is between 1/2 - 2 inches, but it can grow as tall as 4 inches. The cap measures approximately 1/2 to 2 inches wide.

STEM: The stem measures 1 to 4 inches tall and 1/2 to 4 inches wide. The stem is usually shorter than the cap. The stem is finely granular in texture and swollen at the base. The stem is hollow, but sometimes it can be chambered near the bottom. The stem is a pale yellow to tan.

FLESH: it is whitish to pale yellowish or brownish

Look-a-likes: Fortunately, eating most true morels is safe, so the mix-up shouldn't be a severe issue.

Caution: False morels might have wrinkly caps, but they look more like brains than honeycombs. Inspect the mushroom thoroughly before you harvest it, as insects have hollowed out some toxic false morels.

Harvest: Morels grow in the spring, usually between March and late May or early June.

Culinary Uses: Morels are tricky to clean, so you may need to soak them to eliminate dirt, bugs, or other debris. It would be best if you cooked morels, and a great way to get the most out of them is to sauté them in butter.

Medicinal Uses: The use of morels as a medicinal plant dates back centuries. They have been known for their health-related benefits. They have been studied for bioactive properties, including anti-oxidative and anti-inflammatory properties and immunostimulatory and anti-tumor effects.

Witches' Butter

Tremella mesenterica [TRE-MEL-LA MES-EN-TER-I-CA]

While witches' butter isn't known for having much flavor, it is easy to identify and has potentially impressive medicinal properties. Other common names include yellow brain, golden jelly fungus, and yellow trembler, and it is a part of the *Tremellaceae* family.

Look for witches' butter on fallen trees. You'll find yellow witches' butter on downed hardwoods, often acting as a parasite to other mushrooms. Orange witches' butter prefers softwood conifers, particularly those without bark. Despite its ability to bear fruit throughout the year, it is more commonly found in autumn and winter.

Identification: Witches' butter is named such because it looks a bit like butter. Depending on the species, it's either bright orange or yellow. It has a small, jelly-like fruiting body. Witches' butter can be found around the year.

FRUITING BODY: A smooth surface and an irregular shape characterize it. During its wet state, the lobes are tough and greasy or slimy, but they harden as they dry out. As it dries, its color changes from pale yellow to bright orange, then rusty orange when dry.

SPORE: whitish or pale yellow

177

Odor/Taste: bland to none

Look-a-likes: Witches' butter doesn't have any toxic look-a-likes. However, you should always correctly identify a mushroom before eating it. Mushroom poisoning is never fun. As with other wild mushrooms, cook before eating.

Caution: none known

Culinary Uses: Many people eat it primarily for its health benefits, adding it to soups for added nutrition and bulk. It takes on other flavors well.

Medicinal Uses: These include anti-tumor properties and even the potential to improve respiratory health. **It has been researched in several areas and appears effective for treating diabetes, immunomodulatory, and as an anti-microbial.** Tremella mesenterica is traditionally used in Asia as a tonic for lung conditions.

False Chanterelle

Hygrophoropsis aurantiaca [Hɪ-ɢʀᴏ-ꜰᴏʀ-ᴏᴘ-sɪs ᴀᴡ-ʀᴀɴ-ᴛᴇᴇ-ᴀʜ-ᴋᴀ]

The false chanterelle, a wild mushroom, looks remarkably like the much sought-after true chanterelle. It's important to tell them apart, as the false variety isn't as esteemed in the culinary world and might upset the stomach of some. False chanterelles usually have a bright orange to orange-yellow flat or slightly domed cap. The surface of the cap is smooth, often with a wavy or uneven edge. Its gills run down the stem, which is usually yellow and narrows at the base. These mushrooms bear such a strong resemblance to true chanterelles that it can be easy to mix them up. They grow in different forest environments, from pine to hardwood, and are most commonly seen on the forest floor in late summer and fall, right alongside their edible lookalikes. While they're not poisonous, eating false chanterelles can lead to mild stomach problems like nausea, vomiting, and diarrhea. This makes accurate identification crucial. They are often confused with true chanterelles, but the differences are in the gills and stems: true chanterelles have forked, rounded gills and a hollow stem, unlike the false ones.

False Morel

Gyromitra esculenta [ᴊʏ-ʀᴏʜ-MEE-ᴛʀᴜʜ ᴇs-ᴋᴏᴏ-LENT-ᴜʜ]

Be cautious of False Morels, fungi that can easily be confused with the sought-after True Morels due to their similar appearance. However, distinguishing them is vital as False Morels are toxic. These mushrooms feature irregular, brain-like or saddle-shaped caps with wrinkled and lobed surfaces. Their color varies from reddish-brown to dark brown. Unlike True Morels, which have a honeycomb pattern on the cap's interior,

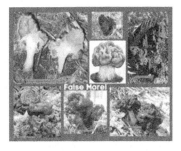

False Morels have a cotton-like or chambered inner structure. They typically thrive in wooded areas during spring and early summer, growing near deciduous trees and conifers in soil rich with decaying organic matter. Found predominantly in temperate regions, consuming False Morels poses serious health risks. They contain gyromitrin, a toxic substance that converts to harmful hydrazine, leading to symptoms like nausea, vomiting, diarrhea, abdominal pain, dizziness, and, in extreme cases, liver and kidney damage, convulsions, or even death.

Lily of the Valley

Convallaria majalis [CON-VA-LAH-REE-UH MUH-JAY-LIS]

Lily of the Valley is a beautiful and delicate plant that might charm your senses with its elegance. However, it's important to be aware of its darker side—it's highly toxic. This plant contains dangerous chemicals known as cardiac glycosides, such as conval-latoxin and convallarin. These substances can seriously affect your heart if consumed, leading to arrhythmias, palpitations, and even cardiac arrest. Beyond its cardiovascular effects, the toxins in Lily of the Valley can cause nausea, vomiting, and severe headaches. So, handling this lovely but hazardous plant with care is vital, keeping it away from children and pets who might stumble upon it.

Poison Hemlock

Conium maculatum [KOH-NEE-UM MAH-KYOO-LAY-TUM]

Poison Hemlock is toxic, and understanding the reasons behind its dangers highlights its risks to both humans and animals. This plant contains a powerful mix of toxic substances, mainly alkaloids, with coniine being the most dangerous. These alkaloids disrupt the normal function of the nervous system, particularly by interfering with neurotransmission at the neuromuscular junctions. Eating Poison Hemlock can cause symptoms

like nausea, vomiting, abdominal pain, paralysis, muscle spasms, and, in severe cases, respiratory failure. It's important to remember that the leaves, stems, seeds, and roots are filled with these dangerous compounds. The extreme toxicity of Poison Hemlock serves as a critical reminder of the importance of accurate identification and the need to avoid this plant when foraging or spending time in areas where it might grow. Confusing it with edible wild plants can lead to severe and potentially deadly consequences.

Poison Sumac

Toxicodendron vernix [Tox-i-co-DEN-dron VER-niks]

This woody shrub can grow up to 20 feet tall and has compound leaves with 7 to 13 leaflets. The leaves are glossy and green in the summer, but they transform into vibrant shades of red and orange in the fall. In late summer, small white or grayish berries appear, serving as a clear warning of its toxicity. Poison sumac prefers damp areas like swamps, bogs, and the edges of streams and ponds. Coming into contact with this plant can result in a painful and itchy rash called allergic contact dermatitis. The rash is caused by urushiol, a toxic oil in leaves, stems, and berries. Symptoms, including redness, blisters, and intense itching, can appear within hours or a few days after exposure. In severe cases, medical attention may be necessary. One of the challenges is distinguishing poison sumac from harmless wetland plants like the white-topped aster and elderberry. Mistaking these look-alikes for poison sumac can lead to accidental contact and subsequent allergic reactions. Therefore, it is crucial to exercise caution and learn to differentiate these plants before exploring wetland areas.

Moonseed

Menispermum canadense [MEN-ih-SPUR-mum kan-uh-DEN-see]

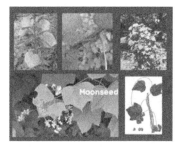

Nestled amidst the wilderness of North America, a lesser-known plant beckons. Moonseed vines, often overshadowed by their more renowned grapevine counterparts, possess an alluring charm with their heart-shaped leaves, greenish-yellow flowers, and peculiar crescent-moon-shaped seeds. Thriving in the moist woodlands, thickets, and the fringes of streams and rivers, moonseed reveals itself as a resilient woody climbing vine. Its glossy green leaves, reminiscent of Valentine hearts, add a touch of elegance to its appearance. As the seasons transition to late spring or early summer, inconspicuous clusters of greenish-yellow flowers grace the plant. Caution must be exercised when encountering Moonseed's treacherous fruit, which resembles grapes. Within a few hours of ingesting Moonseed seeds, one may suffer from nausea, vomiting, abdominal pain, and diarrhea. The toxicity of this plant can escalate to more severe manifestations, including seizures, hallucinations, and damage to vital organs. The danger of Moonseed is further exacerbated by its striking similarity to wild grapes, commonly utilized in creating delectable jams, jellies, and wines. While wild grapes possess spherical seeds, the crescent shape of Moonseed's seeds serves as a telltale sign of danger.

Spotted Spurge

Euphorbia maculata [YOO-FOR-BEE-UH MAK-YOO-LAH-TUH]

Have you ever come across the Spotted Spurge? This little troublemaker, or prostrate or spotted sandmat, is a common weed that loves to make itself at home in gardens, lawns, and disturbed areas all over North America. Don't let its small size fool you - this annual plant is a force to be reckoned with. It's famous for its ability to thrive in all sorts of conditions. The Spotted Spurge is a low-growing weed with oval-shaped leaves that are a vibrant shade of green and adorned with striking red spots. These leaves grow opposite each other along reddish stems, and if you happen to crush them, they release a milky sap that can irritate the skin. This pesky weed is not picky about where it sets up camp - it invades lawns, gardens, and roadside areas. It spreads like wildfire through its seeds, quickly taking over any available space it can find. It forms a dense mat-like growth, smothering nearby plants and competing fiercely for resources. In lawns, it creates unsightly circular patches where the grass is outcompeted and replaced by bare spots. In gardens, it hampers the growth of desirable plants by robbing them of essential nutrients and water. It's important to note that while Spotted Spurge is not edible, it can easily be mistaken for purslane, a succulent and edible plant. To tell them apart, look at the stems - Spotted Spurge has reddish stems, while purslane has green stems. So, be careful not to confuse the two when foraging for edible plants!

PART EIGHT
PREPARING FOR FEAST
OR FAMINE

We could learn a thing or two from nature. Modern life is all about hurrying. Everything has to be quick and convenient, no matter what. Or does it?

"Nature does not hurry, yet everything is accomplished."

-LAO TZU

Foraging is, by definition, a way to connect with nature. So it makes sense to follow those principles when dealing with the gifts it gives us. Proper storage and preservation methods can help us to get the most out of what we forage. When you look after your foraged food, you can enjoy it at your leisure. It's as simple as that. Of course, not every wild edible is equal, so different preservation methods better suit different kinds of food. As usual, I'll break it down into sections so you can reliably preserve and store your foraged bounty.

Greens

Much of what you'll forage in spring will consist of greens when most leafy plants are at their tastiest. Once you start filling your baskets with these delicious leafy greens, you'll likely notice something quickly. Greens take up a lot of space. Not only that but there's so much out there that you can find. So, what do you do with all of these beautiful leaves?

The first thing you should do when you get back home is to put all of those greens in cool water. Not to clean them; although it doesn't hurt, soaking them in water refreshes them. Most edible greens are best when eaten immediately, ideally the same day you've harvested them. If you're dealing with delicate spring greens, stick them in a salad and enjoy the full glory of foraging there and then. But you will usually find other, hardier greens as you also forage. These will last longer and are usually best when cooked. It's still best to act quickly to get the most out of them.

Make sauces and soups, or put them into stews. If you plan on waiting a few days before cooking your greens, or if they're very bitter, you should consider blanching.

Blanching

Blanching is an excellent method to cook large quantities of greens, take the edge off bitter greens, or preserve their color and flavor. Blanched greens will last longer in the refrigerator and can be frozen, letting you store them for ages.

Grab your largest pot and fill it with salted water to quickly blanch many greens. Salt is essential both for its taste and for its preservation properties. Bring this to a boil. Meanwhile, get a large, clean bowl or container and fill it with cold water, ideally with ice. Once your pot of water is bubbling away, cook the greens in large batches until it's wilted. This will take only a few seconds, so be ready to immediately transfer them into the container of cold water until they cool. You can use them as you wish or keep them in the refrigerator until ready. If you want to freeze them, squeeze out the excess water and form them into balls. Put them in the freezer and enjoy all that space you've saved.

An alternative to blanching is freeze-wilting. If your greens are delicate, such as herbs, or you're worried about them losing flavor, you can quickly wilt them in the freezer. Put your greens into a container and put it in the freezer for 30 minutes. Then take it out and let it thaw. This wilts the greens like blanching, and you can either use them or refreeze them.

Dehydration

Dehydration is a great way to preserve your foraged foods for longer. Depending on the greens, you can dehydrate them to turn them into tea blends or use them as herbs. Remember, you can find things in the wild that you won't spot in the grocery store, so you can use these herbs to create unique flavors in your cooking.

There are a few primary methods to dehydrate greens and herbs. The easiest way is to air dry them; this works well with large, thick-stemmed herbs like sage. Arrange them in a bundle and tie the stems together at the bottom with a rubber band. Hang them upside down using butcher's twine or a hook and leave them in a dry place with good air circulation.

Another option is to lay them out flat on a wire rack that allows air to circulate. They should dry after about a week or so.

If you want to speed things up, lay the herbs on a paper towel and put them in the microwave for about 3 minutes. Check on them regularly to ensure they don't burn, but they should dry out nicely. If you have a dehydrator, dry the herbs at 95°F for 2-4 hours or until they crumble in your hands. Once the leaves are dried, store them in a glass jar in the cupboard until ready to use them.

Berries

There's nothing quite like perfectly fresh berries, sweet and juicy. From summer into fall, nature provides plenty of these berries. However, berries have a terrible habit of spoiling relatively quickly, especially in warm weather.

The good news is that there are some steps you can take to keep them deliciously fresh for longer.

As with greens, it's best to process your berry harvest immediately. Cleaning them will eliminate anything that would speed up the spoilage process.

You can fill a large bowl with 3 cups of water and 2 tablespoons of white vinegar (multiply for larger quantities of berries). Sort through the berries, removing debris or spoiled fruit, then put them into the bowl and soak them for up to 10 minutes, stirring occasionally. Then drain into a colander and rinse the berries under cold running water. Dry the berries using a salad spinner or a dishtowel, then store them in a container lined with paper towels. They should keep in the refrigerator for more extended.

FREEZING. Lay the berries in a single layer on a lined, rimmed baking sheet. Pop them in the freezer for a few hours or until frozen solid. Then transfer them to freezer bags, forcing out excess air before returning them to the freezer. This method ensures that the berries freeze separately, making them easier to utilize in future projects.

CANNING. First, put the cleaned berries in a cheesecloth. Then blanch them in boiling water for 30 seconds. The cheesecloth makes it easier to remove them quickly. Loosely fill a canning jar with the fruit, then process them in a boiling water bath for 15 minutes. They should last unopened for a year.

DEHYDRATION. If you're dealing with larger berries or fruit, cut them in half or slices (aim for ¼-inch pieces). Arrange them on dehydrator trays and set the temperature to 135°F. Dry for 10-14 hours or until completely dry. Once they're cool and dry, store them in an airtight container. If you're worried about residual moisture, condition the berries by only partially filling jars and shaking them daily for a week. If condensation appears, dehydrate the berries for a few more hours and then store them properly.

Roots

Root vegetables have a longer shelf life than greens or soft fruits, but you must store them correctly to ensure they last longer. One great way to keep large roots is to layer them in containers with damp sand, sawdust, or potting mix, topping them with the packing material. Then put this container somewhere cool and dark, but they won't freeze. This storage method is best with large, perfect root vegetables. In cool weather, they should last for weeks or even months. Check for rot or growth each week or so.

Suppose the roots are damaged or otherwise imperfect. In that case, It's best to either use them as quickly as possible or dry them and reconstitute them later. Depending on the root, dehydrate them and turn them into powder for flavoring or even in a tea blend.

If you plan on drying roots, wash and scrub them as soon as possible. If you need to, then peel them. Next, chop or slice them into equal pieces. You can air dry them on a wire rack, dehydrate them at 200°F for a couple of hours (checking often) or put them in a dehydrator at 140°F for 8-10 hours or until dry. It can depend on the root. You can store them as they are or blitz them into powder.

Nuts

Most wild-harvested nuts can be stored for months if you keep them correctly. You can follow this method for almost any nut you forage. However, some are trickier than others (black walnuts and their infamous staining juice, for example).

Once you've foraged the nuts, you need to remove the husks. Depending on the nut, this can be as simple as peeling them off, perhaps with a knife, or it may take a while.

After removing the husks, spread the nuts out in a shady, well-circulated area and let them dry for a few days. Put them somewhere that squirrels and other critters can't get them.

Next, put the dried nuts in the freezer for 48 hours, killing off bugs or eggs.

You can store nuts in or out of the shell. They usually last longer in the shells, but they're more convenient when out of the shell. If you take the time to shell them now, you can chuck out any bad ones, saving yourself from future disappointment.

Store them in an airtight container and put them somewhere cool and dry. You can freeze them for more extended storage. Generally, shelled nuts will last for three months at room temperature, six months in the refrigerator, and over a year in the freezer. If they're stale but not rotten, roast them for 10 minutes in a hot oven.

PART NINE
BONUS RECIPES
23 OF MY FAVORITES - JUST FOR YOU

Nannyberry - Maple Butter

Nannyberries' fleshy, paste-like quality makes them an excellent option for a delicious fruit spread. This recipe combines the puree with maple syrup for an even sweeter flavor. You can use it as a spread or use it in baking.

Ingredients:

- 10 cups of Nannyberries
- 7 cups of water
- 1 cup of maple syrup
- ¼ teaspoon of cinnamon
- ¼ teaspoon of salt

Method:

1. Wash the berries and drain, then add to a saucepan with water.
2. Simmer, covered, on low heat for up to 45 minutes, periodically mashing it up to make a puree. Add more water if necessary; if it's too watery, cook it down later.
3. Pass the mixture through a food mill or a fine-mesh sieve.
4. Measure out 5 cups of Nannyberry puree and add it to a blender with maple syrup, cinnamon, and salt. Blitz to make it smooth. Taste to check the seasoning.
5. Pour the butter into a shallow pan and bake for 30 minutes at 325°F or until thick.
6. Store in the refrigerator or freeze.

Notes:

Taste the puree before adding the maple syrup to know how much you need. It may already be sweet enough.

Beach Plum Jelly

If you don't have time to make jelly when you pick the fruits, you can make the juice and freeze it until you're ready. This is also a good trick for spreading the jelly between years of plenty. Makes 7 or 8 (8-ounce) jars

Ingredients:

- 8 heaping cups of beach plums
- 1 cup water
- 6 cups sugar
- 1 package Certo (or 3 ounces liquid pectin)

Method:

1. In a large soup pot, cook the beach plums and the water over medium-high heat until the fruit is soft.
2. Set a large mixing bowl underneath a colander and pour the hot juice through, straining out the pits and skins.
3. Measure out 4 cups of beach plum juice. Rinse out the pot and pour in the liquid with the sugar.
4. Heat the mixture over medium-high heat, stirring until the sugar is dissolved, and bring it to a rolling boil.
5. Add the Certo (or the liquid pectin, if that's what you're using) and bring the mixture back to a boil for 1 minute.
6. Remove the jelly from the heat and pour it into sterilized jars. Store in a cool, dark place for up to a year.

Berry Jam

One fantastic way to preserve berries is to turn them into jam. The best thing is that jam doesn't have to be a production; you can have a batch of berries turned into tasty jam within half an hour. You can then store the jam in the refrigerator or can it for long-term storage.

Ingredients:

- 6 cups of berries
- 2 cups of sugar (or more if you like it even sweeter)
- 2 tablespoons of lemon juice

Method:

1. Put a ceramic plate or dish in the freezer.
2. Put the ingredients into a large saucepan and bring to a boil over medium-high heat.
3. Once it's boiling, reduce the heat and cook uncovered for 20 minutes or until thick. Stir frequently.
4. To test the thickness, then put some jam on the frozen dish. It should be set when exposed to the cold if it doesn't, cook for a bit longer and test again.

Transfer to a sterilized jar and store in the refrigerator. You can also can the jars for 10 minutes in a boiling water bath.

Raspberry Syrup

This simple syrup goes wonderfully with desserts and in beverages, both alcoholic and otherwise. You can combine it with soda water for a simple and tasty summer drink. Ingredients:

- 1½ cups of raspberries, rinsed
- 1 cup of granulated sugar
- 1 cup of water

Method:

1. Combine the water and sugar in a saucepan and bring to a simmer until the sugar has dissolved.
2. Stir in the raspberries and mix with a wooden spoon, mashing the berries.
3. Take the mixture off the heat and let it steep for at least 1 hour.
4. Strain the syrup and put it into sterilized bottles. Store in refrigerator.

Elderberry Liqueur

You can use this recipe with any berries, but elderberries provide a wonderfully mature port-like flavor. They're also full of antioxidants, so you can pretend it's healthy.

Ingredients:

- 1 pint of fresh elderberries, stems removed
- 1 quart of vodka
- 3 inches of lemon rind, white pith removed
- 2 tablespoons of sugar, or more to taste

Method:

1. Wash and sort through the elderberries, remove as many stems as possible, and put them into a quart mason jar. Add the lemon rind and pour over the vodka.
2. Seal and store in a dark cupboard for at least a month(ideally 2 or 3) or up to a year.
3. Pour the vodka through a cheese-cloth lined strainer into another jar and add the sugar. Return to the cupboard and leave it for another week or until the sugar has dissolved.

Enjoy.

nfused Dandelion Vinegar

If you've picked some early spring dandelions, then this simple infused vinegar is a great way to preserve it and create a subtly sweet and bitter salad dressing. It's also highly nutritious and carries some of the health benefits of dandelions. Ingredients:

1¾ cups of fresh dandelion flowers

1½ cups of vinegar (white wine and cider vinegar work well)

Method:

1. Rinse the dandelions and put them into a pint jar.
2. Cover the dandelions with vinegar.
3. Close the jar lid and let it sit somewhere cool for between a week and six weeks. The longer you leave it, the more potent it will be.

When you're happy with it, strain out the flowers and store the infused vinegar in a sealed jar or bottle.

Purple Dead Nettle Tea

If you get a chance to pick those beautiful purple heads of the purple dead nettle, you can use them to make a simple spring tea that's great for allergies.

Ingredients

- 3-4 purple dead nettle heads, rinsed
- 1 cup of boiling water Honey, to taste

Method:

1. Put the purple dead nettle heads into a teapot and pour in the water. Multiply the recipe for more cups.
2. Let steep for 5 minutes.
3. Strain into a cup and add honey.

Notes:

This tea can be astringent, so you may need a lot of honey.

Use local honey to double up on the allergy treatment.

Frozen Blackberry Yogurt

If you want a quick and semi-healthy dessert, this frozen yogurt is a fantastic option to pull out of the freezer and serve up. It's also a surefire way to impress any guests with minimal effort.

Ingredients:

- 3 cups of blackberries
- 1 cup of golden caster sugar
- 2½ cups of Greek yogurt
- ½ cup of honey
- 1 cup of goat's milk (see notes)

Method:

1. Toss the blackberries and sugar in a large bowl and leave for30 minutes. When the fruit starts to break down, mash the berries.
2. In another bowl, combine the other ingredients.
3. Spoon the yogurt into a freezable container, then swirl in the broken-up berries.
4. Freeze for 2 hours, then stir once more and return to the freezer for at least another 3 hours or until frozen.
5. Remove from the freezer a few minutes before serving to soften up.

Notes: You can use cow's milk, but it isn't as tangy.

Shagbark Hickory Syrup

Ingredients:

- 1 pound Shagbark hickory Bark, broken into 4–6-inch pieces
- Cane sugar
- Corn syrup
- Water

Method:

1. Using a stiff brush, scrub the bark well under running water. Make sure you remove any insects, dirt, or bits of lichen that might have made it past your first inspection—Pat the bark dry with a clean dish towel.
2. Spread the clean bark onto a baking sheet. Heat your oven to 325 degrees and roast the bark for 25-30 minutes until it takes on a toasty brown color and you can smell the spicy aroma.
3. Place the roasted bark in a large pot. Cover with cold water, about a gallon. Over medium-high heat, bring the water to a light boil, then reduce the heat and simmer the bark for 30 minutes. Remove the pot from heat and allow it to cool.
4. Remove the bark and filter the water through cheesecloth to remove any bits of bark that might be left over.
5. Measure the amount of hickory tea left from the process. Measure 80% by volume in cane sugar. Add enough corn syrup to the sugar to equal the volume of water. If desired, you can use pure can sugar and eliminate the corn syrup, but the syrup acts as insurance to keep the finished syrup from crystalizing in the refrigerator. If your syrup crystalizes over time, heat the jar in a pan of warm water.
6. Heat the hickory water to a boil, then add the sugar and syrup blend. Stir well to dissolve every crystal of sugar. This is important; even a few undissolved sugar crystals can make your finished syrup crystalize over time. Continue boiling the mixture until the syrup thickens, about 225 degrees Fahrenheit on a candy thermometer, and the total amount of liquid has reduced by 25-30%.
7. Sterilize canning jars (half-pint or pint) by placing a wire rack in the bottom of a large pot. Place the jars upright on the wire rack and fill them with hot water an inch above the jar level. Bring to a boil and continue boiling for 10 minutes.
8. In a separate pot, cover clean rings and new canning lids with water and bring to a light simmer. Simmer for 10 minutes and remove from heat. Transfer the sterilized jars, turned upside down, along with the lids and rings, to a clean wire rack to dry.
9. Pour the hot syrup into the sterilized jars to ½" off the top.
10. Place a jar lid on top and secure it with a ring. As the syrup cools, the cap should seal the jar with an audible pop. After the syrup has cooled

completely, remove the rings and check for a tight seal. The jars of syrup should be shelf stable for a year or more. Refrigerate any open or unsealed jars for up to several months.

11. Use the hickory syrup anywhere you would use maple syrup. As a topping for pancakes, waffles, hot biscuits, cornbread, as a glaze on meat, or add to your favorite cocktails for a sweet and smoky flavor you won't find anywhere else.

Shaggy Mane Ink

One of the unique things about ink cap mushrooms is that you can end up with a black goop that can be turned into ink or puree. While this sounds unappetizing, it's edible and quite pleasant, with a surprisingly mild mushroom flavor. It can create unique-looking dishes, like pasta with black ink sauce and mushroom risotto.

Just have some fun with it.

Ingredients:

- 8 ounces fresh shaggy mane mushrooms, cleaned ¼ teaspoon salt
- 1 medium shallot, finely chopped
- 1 clove of garlic, minced
- 2 tablespoons + ½ tablespoon of neutral oil Splash of white wine or vermouth

Method:

1. Clean the shaggy manes and chop them before putting them in a nonreactive container with a lid. Depending on the temperature, either leave the mushrooms on the counter or store them in the refrigerator.
2. Allow the mushrooms to break down, stirring with a clean spoon every day until they form an inky black mixture. This will take a few days.
3. Once the mixture looks right, sweat the shallot and garlic with a bit of oil until it's translucent. Add the wine, then the mushrooms, and bring to a boil. Cover, then turn down the heat and cook for 10 minutes. If it starts to dry out, add some water.
4. Use a stick blender to puree the mixture while drizzling in the oil. Again, add a little water if it's too thick. Transfer the mixture to a container and store it for up to a week.

Pawpaw Bread

Banana bread is popular among kids and adults alike. It's sweet, comforting, and satisfying. Pawpaw bread is similar, but it also has a unique tropical twist.

Ingredients:

- 2½ cups of flour
- 3 cups of pawpaw pulp/custard (or mashed banana)
- 2 cups of sugar
- 1 cup of butter, softened
- 4 eggs
- ½ teaspoon of vanilla extract
- 2 teaspoons of baking soda
- ¼ teaspoon of salt
- Butter, for greasing

Method:

1. Preheat the oven to 350°F. Grease 2 standard loaf tins and set aside.
2. Whisk together the flour, baking soda, and salt in a bowl.
3. Cream the butter and sugar until light and fluffy, then beat in the eggs one at a time. Add the vanilla and pawpaw and mix.
4. Put the dry ingredients with the wet and mix until the flour is just incorporated.
5. Paw the batter into the tins and bake for 45-60 minutes until the cake is browned and easily lifts away from the sides of the tin. Let cool for 15 minutes in the pan, then remove and enjoy.

Strawberry and Japanese Knotweed Crisp

This sweet dessert has a satisfying crunch, making it a delightful treat for children and adults alike. Ingredients:

- 3 cups of knotweed, washed and diced
- 1 pound of strawberries, diced
- 1 cup of white sugar
- ½ cup of melted butter or neutral oil 1 cup of brown sugar
- 1 cup + 3 tablespoons of flour
- 1 cup old-fashioned rolled oats
- ½ cup of finely chopped walnuts (or other nuts of your choice)

Method:

1. Preheat the oven to 375°F.
2. Put the strawberries, knotweed, white sugar, and 3 tablespoons of flour in a bowl and mix with a spatula until thoroughly combined. Transfer to a 13x9 inch casserole dish and spread, so it's even.
3. Combine the butter/oil with the brown sugar in a bowl. Then add the flour, oats, and walnuts and mix. Distribute the topping evenly over the fruit.
4. Put in the oven and bake for 45 minutes until the top is golden brown and the fruit is bubbling. Enjoy with ice cream.

Pickled Hen of the Woods

If you get a good haul of mushrooms, pickling is a great way to preserve them for future use. Pickle younger specimens and either eat them as a snack or use them to substitute mushrooms in other dishes.

Ingredients:

- 1 pound of young hen of the wood's mushrooms
- 3 cups of water
- 1½ teaspoons of salt
- 2 large cloves of garlic
- Sprigs of fresh thyme (or other woody herbs)
- 2 dried bay leaves
- 1 cup of white wine vinegar (or cider vinegar)

Method:

1. Trim and clean the mushrooms and separate them into small, bitesize leaves.
2. Bring the water, salt, garlic, and herbs to a boil in a pot. Add the mushrooms and cook for 5-10 minutes or until thoroughly cooked.
3. Add the vinegar.
4. Pack sterilized jars with the mushrooms, then top them off with the pickling liquid and seal them. Process in a water bath canner for 15 minutes if you want. Otherwise, store it in the refrigerator.

Pickled Rosehips

You can make syrup or tea with your rosehips, but this pickle is a great way to let them shine. It goes wonderfully with strong cheeses or meat, so add it to your charcuterie board. Ingredients:

- 2 cups of rosehips
- 1 cup of sugar
- ½ cup of cider vinegar
- 1 cup of water
- 6 juniper berries
- 6 cloves
- 2 tablespoons of yellow mustard seeds
- 3 bay leaves
- ½ teaspoon of salt

Method:

1. Cut the rosehips in half, lengthwise. De-seed, then rinse and strain them.
2. Put the sugar in saucepan and the rest of the ingredients, then simmer for 30 minutes, skimming off any foam as you go.
3. Put the pickle into sterilized jars and seal them.

Stir-Fried Greens

You can use this recipe for any slightly bitter greens, making it a beautiful side dish. You can also toss the fried greens with pasta and parmesan, add them to an omelet, or throw them on top of a pizza for a quick, healthy, and tasty meal. Good options include dandelion leaves, garlic mustard, fiddleheads, and plantain.

Ingredients:

- 3-4 cups of washed greens (either fresh or blanched)
- 1-2 cloves of garlic, minced
- ½ teaspoon of red pepper flakes
- 1 tablespoon of olive oil
- Salt and pepper to taste Lemon (optional)

Method:

1. Heat the olive oil on low in a skillet and add the garlic and red pepper flakes. Don't let the garlic brown.
2. When the garlic is soft and everything smells fantastic, turn the heat up and add the greens.
3. Stir the greens, so they're coated with the oil, and keep stirring until they're wilted. This may take about 5-10 minutes.

Serve immediately with salt and pepper and a fresh squeeze of lemon juice.

Porcini Risotto

Ingredients:

- ½ pound of fresh porcini mushrooms, diced
- 5 tablespoons of butter, divided
- 1 shallot, finely diced
- 1 garlic clove, minced
- 2 cups of risotto rice
- ¼ cup of dry white wine or vermouth 1 quart of stock
- ¼ cup of grated parmesan cheese
- ½ teaspoon of dried thyme Salt and pepper, to taste

Method:

1. Keep the quart of stock warm in a saucepan.
2. Heat 3 tablespoons of butter in a large pot over medium heat until it melts. Add the shallot and mushrooms. Sprinkle with salt and sauté for 6-8 minutes, or until the liquid in the mushrooms has boiled away.
3. Stir in the garlic and the rice. Sauté for a few minutes until fragrant, then add the thyme and optional porcini powder.
4. Pour the wine/vermouth into the pot and stir until it evaporated, then add 1 cup of stock.
5. Stir the risotto constantly, adding stock as it gets soaked into the rice. If you run out of stock, then use water. Continue until the rice is cooked but not mushy.
6. Add the remaining 2 tablespoons of butter, cheese, and a little water.
7. Serve immediately and top with a generous amount of fresh black pepper.

B utternut Pesto Pasta

Ingredients:

- 1 pound Pasta, any short kind, like Farfalle
- 1 scant cup White Walnut, raw, about 3 oz.
- 1 small Clove of Garlic, peeled
- 1 ounce Parmigiano-Reggiano cheese, in chunks
- 1 slice of white bread
- 1/2 cup Milk (any fat percentage)
- 4 tablespoons Extra-virgin Olive Oil
- 2 tablespoons Ricotta cheese
- 1/4 teaspoon Salt
- 1 sprig of Marjoram, leaves only, optional
- 4-6 tablespoons Parmigiano-Reggiano cheese, finely grated, to pass at the table
- Freshly ground black pepper to taste

Method:

1. Cook the pasta in a large pot of boiling salted water, occasionally stirring, until tender but still al dente or firm to the bite. Meanwhile...
2. Place the walnuts, chunks of Parmigiano-Reggiano cheese, and garlic in a food processor and grind until it forms a thick paste.
3. Soak the slice of bread in the milk
4. Add the bread and the milk to the food processor, together with the remaining ingredients (but not the grated Parmigiano-Reggiano).
5. Blend until it forms a smooth sauce, scraping the sides occasionally with a spatula (silicone works best).
6. Drain the pasta, reserving 1/2 cup of the cooking water. Return the pasta to the cooking pot and toss immediately with the sauce. Add some of the reserved pasta water if the dish seems too dry. Serve hot, passing some finely grated Parmigiano-Reggiano cheese.

Jerusalem Artichoke Soup

This simple, creamy soup is the perfect comfort meal and a great way to use your Jerusalem artichoke harvest. It lets the flavor of the tubers shine.

Ingredients:

- 2 tablespoons of butter 1 large onion, chopped
- 2 stalks of celery, chopped
- 2 large cloves of garlic, chopped
- 2 pounds of Jerusalem artichokes, peeled and chopped
- 1 quart of chicken/vegetable stock
- Salt and freshly ground black pepper to taste

Method:

1. Sauté the onions and celery for five minutes in the butter, then add the garlic. Don't let anything brown; just cook until soft and fragrant.
2. Add the Jerusalem artichokes and the stock and simmer, covered, for 45 minutes to an hour or until they break down.
3. Use a stick blender to puree the soup—season, taste, and serve.

Chicken Ginseng Soup

Ingredients:

- 1 whole chicken
- 1 medium ginseng roots
- 2 inches of ginger root, sliced
- 20 jujube berries (see notes)
- 2 tablespoons of goji berries
- ½ cup of cooking rice wine (see notes)
- Water
- 1 teaspoon of sea salt

Method:

1. Break the chicken into pieces, then put it into a large pot. Fill the pot with water and bring it to a boil. Let it boil for a couple of minutes, then discard the water. Get rid of any scum on the chicken and in the pot.
2. Put the chicken and 10 cups of water into a large pot. Add the ginger and ginseng roots. Bring to a boil, then simmer with the lid on for 1 hour.
3. Remove the ginseng roots and slice them before adding them back to the pot. Add the jujubes and simmer for another 30 minutes.
4. Put the cooking wine, goji berries, and salt into the pot. Simmer for another 15 minutes, then serve.

Notes:

If you can't get jujube berries, then a couple of tablespoons of dried apple pieces will provide a similar flavor. You can replace cooking rice wine with sherry or vermouth. The pre-boiling of the chicken isn't strictly necessary, but it will give a clearer broth.

Creamy Fiddlehead Soup with Chives

Makes 6 servings

Ingredients:

- 1-pound fresh Ostrich Fern/Fiddleheads
- 1 tbsp butter
- 2 spring onions sliced (reserve the greens for garnish)
- 1 clove garlic minced
- 1 cups chicken stock
- 1 dried bay leaf
- 1 medium potato cut into 1/4-inch cubes
- 1 cup heavy cream
- 1/4 cup chopped chives
- 1/2 tsp. kosher salt
- 1/4 teaspoon ground black pepper

Method:

1. Rinse and clean Fiddleheads well in cold water to remove the brown skin. Drain and set aside
2. Melt butter in a large saucepan over medium-high heat.
3. Add the Spring onions and sauté until fragrant and tender, about 3 minutes.
4. Add the garlic and cook for roughly 1 minute more.
5. Pour in the chicken stock, add the bay leaf, and bring to a boil over medium-high heat.
6. Add the Fiddleheads and potatoes. Lower the heat and simmer until the vegetables are tender: roughly 15 minutes.
7. Add the heavy cream, chives, salt, and pepper. Simmer while stirring until slightly thickened.
8. Serve warm and garnish with green onions.

Old-Fashioned Black Walnut Cookies

Ingredients:

- 1 cup light brown sugar
- 1/2 cup (4 ounces) unsalted butter, softened 1 large egg
- One teaspoon of pure vanilla extract
- 1 2/3 cups all-purpose flour
- 1/2 teaspoon baking soda
- 1/2 teaspoon salt
- 1 cup black walnuts, chopped
- 1 cup granulated sugar for dipping

Method:

1. Gather the ingredients. Heat the oven to 375 F.
2. Grease a large baking sheet or line it with parchment paper.
3. Cream the brown sugar and butter in a mixing bowl with an electric mixer until light. Add egg and vanilla; beat well.
4. In another bowl, combine the dry ingredients—flour, baking soda, and salt —and mix to blend well.
5. Add the flour mixture to the creamed mixture along with the black walnuts; mix well.
6. Shape the dough into small balls about the size of walnuts.
7. Dip the cookie balls in sugar. Place them on the prepared cookie sheet and press with the bottom of a glass to flatten slightly.

Bake in a preheated oven for 12 to 15 minutes.

Burdock Root Decoction for dogs

Combine 1 cup cold water and 1 to 2 teaspoons dried or 2 tablespoons fresh burdock root. Cover and bring to a boil. Reduce heat and simmer for 15-20 minutes.

Remove from heat and let stand an additional 10 minutes. Strain and store in a container with a tight lid.

Dosage: Add up to 1 teaspoon of the decoction per 10 pounds of body weight to your dog's food daily.

Black Trumpet Soufflé

You can do many things with black trumpets' delicate, smoky flavor. This soufflé is surprisingly simple to make, considering how decadent the result is. Ingredients:

- 3-5 ounces of black trumpet mushrooms
- 3-5 ounces of button mushrooms
- ¼ cup of butter
- ½ cup of flour
- 1¼ cup of milk
- ½-¾ cup of grated Swiss cheese
- 3 eggs
- Salt and pepper to taste

Method:

1. Preheat the oven to 350°F. Sauté the mushrooms in the butter for a few minutes.
2. Add the flour and stir together for 2 minutes.
3. Remove from the heat and slowly pour in the milk, stirring constantly.
4. Add the cheese and the salt and pepper.
5. Separate the eggs, then beat the egg yolks into the mixture.
6. Whisk the egg whites and add them to the mixture.
7. Pour everything into a soufflé dish and bake for 30-40 minutes.

CONCLUSION

'm a big fan of foraging if you haven't figured it out. This book includes the most delectable delights of the Mid-Atlantic, but believe it or not, there is more to discover. There are more edible plants, mushrooms, and many more recipes. Foraging is, simply put, fantastic. Let me break it down for you.

First, foraging is free. You get to save money on groceries because you're finding what you need in nature. It's all there for the taking; you must get out and take it. Plus, the food is right on your doorstep, and the things you find are packed with nutrients. It's a fantastic way to live a sustainable life. You can use it in your cooking or make medicines and tinctures to boost your health. There's no shipping, no processing, and you pick it at its freshest and best, without any intervention by other humans. This means you can try new flavors you'd never experience by sticking to what you can purchase at the grocery store. Even better, you get to cook to impress. It's one thing to tell someone that you made a tasty meal from scratch, but it's a whole other level if you've foraged the food on top of it.

There's nothing quite like going out into the wilderness and finding the food that reconnects you with nature. You can learn about nature while exploring new places while searching for new goodies. Getting out there isn't just fun, but it's a fantastic way to get some much-needed fresh air, sunshine, and exercise.

Foraging doesn't just allow you to connect with nature, either. While you can forage alone, it can be a fantastic social activity. There's a reason why I've mentioned finding local foraging groups so often. Yes, foraging with a guide is always beneficial, especially if you're a beginner. You can also meet new people and forge long-lasting friendships with people who care about the same things you do. Foraging is also a brilliant family activity. You can go out there with your friends and family, find something extraordinary, then return home and turn it into a treat you all enjoy. That's a perfect day right there.

I've been fortunate enough to catch the foraging bug decades ago and have had the opportunity to explore various places and foods. I've found wild edibles in urban, suburban, and rural areas, and it's been a wealth of fun and good eating.

I still remember when I saw my first morel mushroom. It was a lonely mushroom, but getting home, slicing it in half, and frying it in butter was a surprisingly exciting experience. It was a new flavor and experience, inspiring me to find more delicious treats like them. As you get more experienced, you'll find more things and learn how to make the most of them. Once you start, you'll never look back.

So, do me a favor and get out there. See what you find. As usual, I'll give you a quote to think about in the meantime.

"Forget not that the earth delights to feel your bare feet and the winds long to play with your hair."

- **KHALIL GIBRAN,** LEBANESE-AMERICAN WRITER, POET AND VISUAL ARTIST

PART TEN
APPENDIX

THE UNIVERSAL EDIBILITY TEST

When you're in an unfamiliar area or dealing with a survival situation, it can be challenging to distinguish between edible and non-edible plants. That's where the universal edibility test becomes invaluable. Its purpose is to help you determine the edibility of a plant. However, it's important to note that this test should only be considered a last resort. Ideally, it would be best if you always strived to find plants or mushrooms that you can confidently identify as safe to eat. This becomes especially crucial when foraging and coming across an edible plant you've never encountered before.

This scenario is bound to happen to everyone at some point. Even if you're confident in identifying edible plants, it's always wise to exercise caution and try a small amount first. Even if a plant is generally safe, it may not agree with your digestion. Trying a new food and realizing it doesn't sit well with you after consuming a large portion can be quite unpleasant. Moreover, there's always a chance of having an undiagnosed food allergy. Imagine consuming a significant quantity of plant food on an empty stomach; it can lead to cramps, nausea, diarrhea, or other gastrointestinal issues. An upset stomach can quickly turn an otherwise enjoyable foraging trip into a regretful experience.

Step 1: Fast for eight hours. You likely haven't eaten for at least eight hours in a survival situation like this. Still, it's essential to start on an empty stomach so that you know whether or not the plant you are testing is what has made you unwell. You can and should drink plenty of clean water, if possible.

Step 2: Check for common poisonous traits. Most toxic plants have distinguishing characteristics that are unlikely to be found on edible plants. These include shiny, waxy leaves, spines, fine hairs, milky sap, umbrella-shaped flowers, and green or white berries. If it looks like dill or parsley, avoid it, and steer clear of anything that smells like almonds. Not every plant with these characteristics is toxic; edible dandelions have milky sap, for example, but it's an excellent rule of thumb. Rule out anything with those traits.

Step 3: Once you find a plant without any of those traits, ensure you can find plenty of specimens. Remember, the edibility test takes time, so there's not much point in going through the whole process if you can't find any more plants of that type. When you find a likely plant, break it down into separate sections: flower, leaf, stem, etc. Not every plant part is edible, even if one part is. For example, potato tubers are edible, but the plant's stem is toxic. You will need to test every aspect of the plant individually.

Step 4: Now, it's time to start testing. Select a plant part and rub it on your skin. Most people rub it on their inner forearm, the inside of their elbow, or their outer lip. Wait for fifteen minutes. Continue with the test if you don't experience tingling, burning, or other adverse reactions. If any of the above persist, you will want to choose a different plant part.

Step 5: If all is well from the step above, do a taste test with the same plant part. Put it in your mouth and don't chew or swallow; leave it for five minutes. Spit it out and wash your mouth if you have any adverse reactions. Do the same if you taste bitterness, soapy flavors, or experience numbness. If nothing happens, continue with the test.

Step 6: Do a more extensive taste test. Put the plant part in your mouth and chew for five minutes. Wait for any of the adverse effects mentioned above and spit out excess saliva (don't swallow anything yet). If everything seems okay after five minutes, swallow the plant part. Now, the waiting begins. You need to fast for another eight hours before the next step.

Step 7: If you haven't experienced any digestive issues, you can prepare and eat one tablespoon of the plant part. If possible, it's usually safer to cook the plant part. If there are no poisoning symptoms after another eight hours of waiting, you can be sure this plant part is edible as you prepared.

GLOSSARY

Plant Families

Actinidiaceae - This flowering plant family has three genera and about 355 species. They consist of shrubs, small trees, and lianas. They are primarily tropical and are particularly common in Southeast Asia.

Anacardiaceae - The cashew or sumac family of flowering plants includes 83 genera and 860 species. Several species bear drupes and sometimes produce *urushiol*, which can cause skin irritation.

Apiaceae - Known as the celery, carrot, and parsley family, or umbellifers, primarily aromatic flowering plants are named after the genus Apium.

Araliaceae - There are approximately 43 genera and about 1500 species of flowering plants in this family, most of these plants are woody, and some are herbaceous.

Asparagaceae - the asparagus family of flowering plants based on the edible garden asparagus, *Asparagus officinalis*.

Aspleniaceae - The spleenwort family **is** a family of ferns

Asteraceae - The Compositae family was first described in the year 1740. They are called daisies, sunflowers, asters, composites, or sunflowers. With more than 32,000 species and 1,900 genera, it is the world's largest flowering plant group, rivaled only by the Orchidaceae family.

Berberidaceae - Generally known as the Barberry family, this group of flowering plants contains 18 genera.

Brassicaceae - These medium-sized flowering plants are economically important. They are commonly known as the mustards, crucifers, or cabbage family.

Caryophyllaceae - The carnation family is a family of flowering plants with about 2,625 known species.

Elaeagnaceae - The Oleaster family comprises small trees and shrubs.

Ericaceae - The heath or heather family consists of flowering plants that flourish in acidic and infertile environments. Cranberries, blueberries, huckleberries, rhododendron (including azaleas), and a wide range of heaths and heathers are examples of well-known members.

Euphorbiaceae - Among flowering plants, the spurge family is one of the largest. They are also commonly known as euphorbias in English, their genus name. Most spurges are herbs, such as Euphorbia paralias, but some are shrubs or trees, particularly in the tropics.

Lamiaceae [LAY-MEE-AY-SEE-EE] The mint or deadnettle family is aromatic in all parts. They include widely used culinary herbs like basil, mint, rosemary, sage, savory, marjoram, oregano, hyssop, thyme, lavender, and perilla. Catnip, salvia, bee balm, wild dagga, and oriental motherwort are medicinal herbs.

Malvaceae - The Mallow family of flowering plants is estimated to contain 244 genera with 4225 known species. Among the well-known members of this plant family are okra, cotton, cacao, and durian.

Menispermaceae - The moonseed family comprises 440 species, most of which are found in low-lying tropical regions, with some species also found in temperate and arid regions.

Morchellaceae -

Oxalidaceae - The wood sorrel family comprises five genera of herbaceous plants, shrubs, and small trees, with about 570 species in the Oxalis genus.

Plantaginaceae - The Plantain family and order Lamiales include common flower species such as snapdragon and foxglove.

Polygonaceae - The knotweed or smartweed-buckwheat family is an informal name for a family of flowering plants. There are about 1200 species within about 48 genera. There are members of this family worldwide, but they are most abundant in the North Temperate Zone.

Portulacaceae - The purslane family is a family of flowering plants with 115 species in one genus, Portulaca.

Ranunculaceae - the buttercup or crowfoot family is a family of over 2,000 known flowering plants in 43 genera distributed worldwide.

Rosaceae - The rose family includes 4,828 species of flowering plants.

Tremellaceae -

Viburnaceae - was previously known as the Adoxaceae family and is commonly known as the Moschatel family. About 150–200 species belong to this family of flowering plants.

Plant Types

Annual [AN-YOO-*UHL*] - Plants without a permanent woody stem. They are usually flowering garden plants or potherbs.

Deciduous [DIH-SIJ-OO-UHS] - After the growing season, the plant sheds leaves and turns dormant.

Dioecious [DAHY-EE-SH*UHS*] - having the male and female organs in separate and distinct individuals, having different sexes.

Herbaceous [HUR-BEY-SH*UHS*] - low-growing plants with soft green stems. Their above-ground growth is often seasonal.

Monoecious [MUH-NEE-SHUHS] - having the stamens and the pistils in separate flowers on the same plant.

Perennial [PUH-REN-EE-UHL] - It usually lasts for more than two years. These plants don't have a lot of woody growth.

Plant Parts

Achene [*UH*-KEEN] - a small, dry one-seeded fruit that does not open to release the seed.

Anther [AN-THER] - the pollen-bearing part of a stamen.

Filament [FIL-*UH*-MUHNT] - the stalklike portion of a stamen, supporting the anther.

Ligulate [LIG-YU*H*-LIT] - strap-shaped, such as the ray florets of daisy family plants.

Peltate [PEL-TEYT] - fixed to the stalk by the center or by some point distinctly within the margin.

Petiole [PET-EE-OHL] - the slender stalk by which a leaf is attached to the stem; leafstalk.

Pistil [PIS-TL] - the ovule-bearing or seed-bearing female organ of a flower, consisting when complete of the ovary, style, and stigma.

Pith [PITH] - The soft central cylinder of tissue in the plant's stem.

Sepal [SEE-P*UHL*] - The outer parts of the flower (often green and leaf-like) that enclose a developing bud.

Sessile [SES-IL] - attached directly by its base without a stalk or peduncle.

Stamen [STEY-MUHN] - the pollen-bearing organ of a flower, consisting of the filament and the anther.

Staminodia [STAM-*UH*-NOH-DEE-*UH*] - A stamen that is sterile or abortive.

Whorled [WURL'D] - The arrangement of like parts around a point on an axis, such as leaves or flowers;

Leaf Types

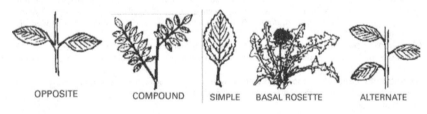

OPPOSITE   COMPOUND   SIMPLE   BASAL ROSETTE   ALTERNATE

Alternate - The leaves are single at each node and spiral upwards along the stem.

Basal Leaf: a leaf that grows lowest on the stem of a plant or flower.

Compound -

Opposite -

Palmate [PAL-MEYT] - Having four or more lobes or leaflets.

Palmately compound - A petiole's tip is attached to a leaflet.

Pinnate [PIN-EYT] - Each side of a stalk is divided into leaflets

Rosette [ROH-ZET] - a circular arrangement of leaves or structures resembling leaves.

Simple - Leaves with a single, undivided lamina

Tripinnately compound - Leaf made up of three pinnate parts.

Leaf Shapes

LANCE-SHAPED ELLIPTIC EGG-SHAPED OBLONG WEDGE-SHAPED TRIANGULAR LONG-POINTED TOP-SHAPED

Cordate [KAWR-DEYT] - heart-shaped.

Elliptical [IH-LIP-TI-KUHL] - Planar, shaped like a flattened circle, symmetrical about the long and short axes, tapering equally to the tip and the base; oval.

Lanceolate [AN-SEE-UH-LEYT] - shaped like the head of a lance, having a rounded base and a tapering apex.

Long-pointed - Lying close and flat and pointing toward the plant's apex or structure.

Oblanceolate [OB-LAN-SEE-UH-LIT] - having a rounded apex and a tapering base.

Oblong [OB-LAWNG]- Having a length a few times greater than the width, with sides almost parallel and ends rounded.

Ovate [OH-VEYT] - egg-shaped, having such a shape with a broader end at the base.

Triangular [TRAHY-ANG-GYUH-LER] - Planar with three sides.

Wedge - narrowly triangular, wider at the apex, and tapering toward the base.

Flower Types

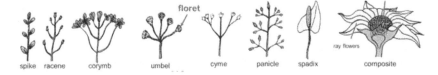

spike racene corymb umbel cyme panicle spadix composite

floret

ray flowers

Corymb [KAWR-IMB] - a form of inflorescence in which the flowers form a flat-topped or convex cluster, the outermost flowers being the first to open.

Composite [KUHM-POZ-IT] is characterized by alternate, opposite, or *whorled* leaves and a whorl of bracts surrounding its flower heads. These flower heads typically extend from a disk containing tiny petal-less flowers and from the disk's rim to a ray of petals.

Cyme [SAHYM] - an inflorescence in which the primary axis bears a single central or terminal flower that blooms first.

Inflorescence [IN-FLAW-RES-UHNS] - the complete flower head of a plant, including stems, stalks, bracts, and flowers.

Panicle [PAN-I-KUHL] - any loose, diversely branching flower cluster.

Raceme [REY-SEEM] - a flower cluster with separate flowers attached by short equal stalks at equal distances along a central stem. The flowers at the base of the main stem develop first.

Spike [SPAHYK] - a type of racemose inflorescence.

Spadix [SPEY-DIKS] - an inflorescence consisting of a spike with a fleshy or thickened axis, usually enclosed in a spathe.

Umbel or Subumbel [UHM-BUHL] - consisting of several short flower stalks that spread from a common point, like umbrella ribs.

Fruit/Berry

Aggregate fruit [AG-RI-GIT FROOT]- composed of a cluster of carpels belonging to the same flower as the raspberry.

Dehiscent [Dɑ'HɪʊSONT] - opens to release seeds or pollen

Drupe [DROOP] - a fleshy fruit with thin skin and a central stone containing the seed, e.g., a plum, cherry, almond, or olive.

Globoid [GLOH-BOID] - approximately globular. Globe-shaped; spherical.

Infructescence [IN-FRUC-TES-CENCE] - an aggregate fruit.

Syconium [SAHY-KOH-NEE-UHM] - a fleshy hollow receptacle that develops into a multifruit.

Bark

221

Acaulescent [AK-AW-LES-UHNT] - stemless

Lenticel [LEN-TUH-SEL] - One of the many holes in a woody plant's stem that allows air to exchange between the inside and outside.

Myrmecochory - the dispersal of fruits and seeds by ants.

Elaiosome - an oil-rich body on seeds or fruits that attracts ants, which act as dispersal agents.

Medical Terms

Amygdalin [UH-MIG-DUH-LIN] - White, bitter-tasting glycosidic powder usually obtained from the leaves and seeds of plants of the genus Prunus and related genera: used mainly as an expectorant in medicine.

Anthocyanins [AN-THUH-SAHY-UH-NIN] - These flavonoids are known for their pigmentation properties, responsible for fruits, vegetables, flowers, and cereals' red, purple, and blue colors.

Astringent [UH-STRIN-JUHNT] - Contracting the body's tissues or canals reduces mucus or blood discharges.

Berberine [BUR-BUH-REEN] - Known as an antipyretic, antibacterial, and stomachic, this crystalline, water-soluble alkaloid is derived from barberry or goldenseal.

Carotenoid [KUH-ROT-N-OID] - Red or yellow pigments, similar to carotene, found in animal fat and some plants.

Cyanogenic glycosides - chemical compounds contained in foods that release hydrogen cyanide when chewed or digested.

Demulcent [DIH-MUHL-SUHNT] - a substance that relieves irritation of the mucous membranes in the mouth by forming a protective film.

Depurative [DEP-YUH-REY-TIV] - herbs considered to have purifying and detoxifying effects.

Flavonoids [FLEY-VUH-NOID] - An antioxidant, antiviral, anticancer, anti-inflammatory, and an anti-allergenic group of water-soluble polyphenols found in plants.

Hydrocyanic acid - scientific word for cyanide.

Lycopene [LAHY-KUH-PEEN] - Red crystalline substance found in some fruits, including tomatoes and paprika.

Odontalgic [OH-DON-TAL-JUH] - toothache.

Prunasin [PRŪ-NƏ-SƏN] - A cyanogenic glucoside related to amygdalin found in Prunus species.

Urolithiasis [YOOR-OH-LI-THAHY-UH-SIS] - A disease where stones form in the urinary tract.

Urushiol [OO-ROO-SHEE-AWL] - The active irritant principle in several plant species in the Rhus genus.

General definitions

Anthropogenic [AN-THRUH-PUH-JEN-IK] - caused by humans.

Glaucous [GLAW-KUHS] - covered with a whitish bloom, as a plum.

Siliceous [SUH-LISH-UHS] - growing in soil rich in silica.

Calcareous [KAL-KAIR-EE-UHS] - occurring on chalk or limestone.

Monoecious [MUH-NEE-SHUHS] - On the same plant, the stamens and pistils are in separate flowers.

Mucilaginous [MYOO-SUH-LAJ-UH-NUHS] - having a viscous or gelatinous consistency.

ABOUT THE AUTHOR

Shannon Warner is a long-time forager and survivalist with a deep love for the outdoors. She has spent countless hours exploring the wilderness, learning about the plants and animals that inhabit it, and honing her skills in sustainable harvesting and ethical foraging. She has embarked on many adventures with her two loyal dogs by her side, from hiking and camping to hunting and fishing.

One of her core beliefs is in sustainable harvesting and ethical foraging. She firmly believes that it is possible to enjoy the bounty of nature without causing harm to the environment or depleting its resources. In her books, she provides practical tips and advice on how to forage in a way that is both sustainable and respectful of the natural world.

Whether you are an experienced forager or a beginner looking to learn more about the plants that grow in your backyard, Shannon's book is an invaluable resource that will inspire and inform you. With her expert guidance, you, too, can discover the many benefits of wild edible plants and unlock the secrets of the natural world.

PLANT INDEX

Allegheny Blackberry_____27

American Beech_____127

American Hazelnut_____129

American Pokeweed_____69

American Red Raspberry_____61

Autumn Olive_____29

Beach Plum_____31

Bearberry_____33

Bitternut Hickory_____131

Black Chanterelle_____151

Black Cherry_____133

Black Cohosh_____71

Black Elderberry_____35

Black Walnut (Eastern)_____135

Blewit_____153

Bloodroot_____73

Blue Violet_____75

Burdock Root_____77

Butternut_____153

Chanterelle_____155

Chickasaw Plum_____39

Chicken of the Woods_____157

Chickweed_____79

Chicory_____81

Chinese Chestnut_____137

Dandelion_____83

Dog Rose_____41

Entoloma_____149

False Chanterelle_____179

False Morel_____179

Garlic Mustard_____85

Giant Puffball_____159

Ginseng_____87

Goldenseal_____89

Hardy Kiwi_____43

Hen of the Woods_____161

Honey Mushroom_____163

Japanese Barberry_____45

Japanese Knotweed_____91

Jerusalem Artichoke_____93

King Bolete_____165

Lily of the Valley_____179

Lobster_____167

Mallow_____95

Moonseed_____181

Mugwort_____97

Nannyberry_____47

Northern Highbush Blueberry_____37

Northern Spicebush_____49

Ostrich Fern_____99

Oyster_____169

Pawpaw_____51

Persimmon_____53

Pineapple weed_____101

Pink Wood Sorrel_____103

Plantain_____105

Poison Hemlock_____179

Poison Sumac_____180

Purple Deadnettle_____107

Purple Passionflower_____55

Purslane_____109

Red Chokeberry_____57

Red Mulberry_____59

Sassafras_____111

Shagbark Hickory_____139

Shaggy Mane_____171

Spotted Spurge_____181

Staghorn Sumac_____113

Watercress_____115

White Button_____173

White Oak_____141

Wild Garlic_____117

Wild Ramp_____119

Wineberry_____65

Witches' Butter_____175

Woodland Strawberry_____63

Yellow Sweetclover_____121

Asimina triloba (L.) Dunal observed in the United States of America by John Hall (licensed under http://creativecommons.org/licenses/by/4.0/)

Diospyros virginiana L. observed in the United States of America by Jacob Saucier (licensed under http://creativecommons.org/licenses/by/4.0/)

Aronia arbutifolia (L.) Pers. observed in the United States of America by Samuel A. Schmid (licensed under http://creativecommons.org/licenses/by/4.0/)

Aronia arbutifolia (L.) Pers. observed in the United States of America by Katja Schulz (licensed under http://creativecommons.org/licenses/by/4.0/)

Morus rubra L. observed in the United States of America by Sam Kieschnick (licensed under http://creativecommons.org/licenses/by/4.0/)

Morus rubra L. observed in the United States of America by Abby Darrah (licensed under http://creativecommons.org/licenses/by/4.0/

Morus rubra L. observed in the United States of America by Lillie (licensed under http://creativecommons.org/licenses/by/4.0/)

Rubus idaeus subsp. *strigosus* (Michx.) Focke observed in the United States of America by Douglas Goldman (licensed under http://creativecommons.org/licenses/by/4.0/)

Rubus idaeus subsp. *strigosus* (Michx.) Focke observed in the United States of America by Elliott Gordon (licensed under http://creativecommons.org/licenses/by/4.0/)

Rubus idaeus subsp. *strigosus* (Michx.) Focke observed in the United States of America by egreten (licensed under http://creativecommons.org/licenses/by/4.0/)

Fragaria virginiana Duchesne observed in the United States of America by Matt Lavin (licensed under http://creativecommons.org/licenses/by/sa-4.0/)

Fragaria virginiana Duchesne observed in the United States of America by Matt Lavin (licensed under http://creativecommons.org/licenses/by/sa-4.0/)

Fragaria virginiana Duchesne observed in the United States of America by Casey H. Richart (licensed under http://creativecommons.org/licenses/by/4.0/)

Rubus phoenicolasius Maxim. observed in the United States of America by Sandy Wolkenberg (licensed under http://creativecommons.org/licenses/by/4.0/)

Rubus phoenicolasius Maxim. observed in the United States of America by Bruce Kirchoff (licensed under http://creativecommons.org/licenses/by/4.0/)

Rubus phoenicolasius Maxim. observed in the United States of America by Lawrence Yang (licensed under http://creativecommons.org/licenses/by/4.0/)

Rubus phoenicolasius Maxim. observed in the United States of America by Scott Morris (licensed under http://creativecommons.org/licenses/by/4.0/)

Phytolacca americana L. observed in the United States of America by Skyler Principe (licensed under http://creativecommons.org/licenses/by/4.0/)

Actaea racemosa L. observed in the United States of America by Theo Rickert (licensed under http://creativecommons.org/licenses/by/4.0/)

Actaea racemosa L. observed in the United States of America by stinger (licensed under http://creativecommons.org/licenses/by/4.0/

Sanguinaria canadensis L. observed in the United States of America by Alexandra Destria (licensed under http://creativecommons.org/licenses/by/4.0/)

Arctium lappa L. observed in the United States of America by Tom Scavo (licensed under http://creativecommons.org/licenses/by/4.0/)

Stellaria media (L.) Vill. observed in the United States of America by giantcicada (licensed under http://creativecommons.org/licenses/by/4.0/)

Stellaria media (L.) Vill. observed in the United States of America by Randy A Nonenmacher (licensed under http://creativecommons.org/licenses/by/4.0/)

Viola sororia Willd. observed in the United States of America by Elliot Greiner (licensed under http://creativecommons.org/licenses/by/4.0/)

Alliaria petiolata observed in the United States of America by Natalie Lemanski (licensed under https://creativecommons.org/licenses/by-sa/4.0/

Alliaria petiolata observed in the United States of America by Deana Tempest Thomas (licensed under https://creativecommons.org/licenses/by-sa/4.0/

Panax quinquefolius L. observed in the United States of America by Tom Scavo (licensed under http://creativecommons.org/licenses/by/4.0/)

Panax quinquefolius L. observed in the United States of America by Tom Scavo (licensed under http://creativecommons.org/licenses/by/4.0/)

Hydrastis canadensis L. observed in the United States of America by Sandra Keller (licensed under http://creativecommons.org/licenses/by/4.0/)

Hydrastis canadensis L. observed in the United States of America by Theo Rickert (licensed under http://creativecommons.org/licenses/by/4.0/)

Gyromitra esculenta (Pers.) Fr. observed in the United States of America by Erlon Bailey (licensed under http://creativecommons.org/licenses/by-sa/4.0/)
Gyromitra esculenta (Pers.) Fr. observed in the United States of America by José Garrido (licensed under http://creativecommons.org/licenses/by/4.0/)

Bibliography

Adamant, A. (2018, August 22). *Foraging Burdock for Food and Medicine.* Practical Self Reliance. Retrieved June 23, 2022, from https://practicalselfreliance.com/edibleburdock/

Adamant, A. (2018, October 11). *Foraging Witch's Butter Mushroom.* Practical Self Reliance. Retrieved June 20, 2022, from https://practicalselfreliance.com/witches-butter/ Adamant, A. (2019, October 15). *Foraging Butter Nuts (Juglans cinerea): Butternut Tree Identification and Processing.* Practical Self Reliance. Retrieved June 13, 2022, from https://practicalselfre liance.com/butternut-juglans-cinerea/

Adamant, A. (2019, December 23). *Foraging Nannyberry (Viburnum lentago).* Practical Self Reliance. Retrieved June 28, 2022, from https://practicalselfreliance.com/nannyberry-viburnum-lentago/

Albers, C. (2018, April 20). *Growing Nut Trees in NYS – CornellForestConnect.* CornellForestConnect. Retrieved June 23, 2022, from https://cornellforestconnect. ning.com/profiles/blogs/growing-nut-trees-in-nys

American ginseng. (n.d.). Wikipedia. Retrieved June 30, 2022, from https://en.wikipedia. org/wiki/American_ginseng

Anderson, T. (2021, October 18). *Foraging and Picking Porcini Mushrooms Safely and How to Dry Them.* Lovely Greens. Retrieved June 25, 2022, from https://lovelygreens.com/ foraging-and-drying-porcini-mushroom-cep-steinpilz/

Any good spots for foraging? : r/WestVirginia. (2019, August 7). Reddit. Retrieved June 29, 2022, from https://www.reddit.com/r/WestVirginia/comments/cn8p5m/ any_good_spots_for_-foraging/

Ballard, L. (2018, November 14). *Forage Wild Nuts for Your Holiday Feast.* Cool Green Science. Retrieved June 27, 2022, from https://blog.nature.org/science/2018/11/14/ forage-wild-nuts-for-your-holi-day-feast/

Bauer, E. (n.d.). *Homemade Sassafras Root Beer Recipe.* Simply Recipes. Retrieved June 10, 2022, from https://www.simplyrecipes.com/recipes/ homemade_sassafras_root_beer/

Bauer, E. (n.d.). *Sunchoke Soup Recipe.* Simply Recipes. Retrieved June 29, 2022, from https://www. simplyrecipes.com/recipes/jerusalem_artichoke_soup/

Bearberry: Pictures, Flowers, Leaves & Identification | Arctostaphylos uva ursi. (n.d.). Edible Wild Food. Retrieved June 15, 2022, from https://www.ediblewildfood.com/ bearberry.aspx

Besemer, T. (2020, April 20). *5 Delicious Recipes For 5 Easy To Forage Plants.* Rural Sprout. Retrieved July 1, 2022, from https://www.ruralsprout.com/easy-foraging-recipes/ *Black Cohosh (Actaea racemosa L.) – Forest Farming.* (2019, August 26). Forest Farming. Retrieved June 30, 2022, from https://forest-farming.extension.org/black-cohoshactaea-racemosa-l/

Brill, S. (n.d.). Wildman Steve Brill: Home. Retrieved June 22, 2022, from https://www. wildmansteve-brill.com/brown, c. (2018, January 9). *The case for legal foraging in Ameri-ca's National Parks.* The Counter. Retrieved June 3, 2022, from https://thecounter.org/the-case-for-legaliz ing-foraging-in-national-parks/

Bussing, K. (2022, May 16). *Can You Eat Dandelions? | How to Cook Dandelions.* Taste of Home. Retrieved June 6, 2022, from https://www.tasteofhome.com/article/how-tocook-dandelions/

Chapin, M., & Demers, A. (n.d.). *Foraging Tours and Classes in West Virginia.* Eat The Planet. Retrieved June 29, 2022, from https://eattheplanet.org/foraging-tours-andclasses-in-west-virginia/

Chickweed Foraging: Identification, look-a-likes, and Uses. (2021, February 11). Grow Forage Cook Ferment. Retrieved June 15, 2022, from https://www.growforagecookferment. com/foraging-for-chickweed/

Contributor, G. (2014, August 13). *Wild Blackberry Season In The Adirondacks - - The Adirondack Almanack.* The Adirondack Almanack -. Retrieved June 22, 2022, from https://www.adirondackalmanack.com/ 2014/08/wild-blackberry-season-in-theadirondacks.html

Cooking And Eating Watercress — WFI. (n.d.). Watercress Farms. Retrieved June 6, 2022, from https:// www.watercressfarms.com/cooking-and-eating-watercress

Costello, I. (2011, June 6). *EDIBLE TRADITIONS: Wild Beach Plums — Edible Boston.* Edible Boston. Retrieved June 15, 2022, from https://www.edibleboston.com/edibleboston/edible-traditions-wild-beach-plums

Cottam, L. (2019, August 5). *Hazelnuts: Where and When to Forage.* Woodland Trust. Retrieved June 9, 2022, from https://www.woodlandtrust.org.uk/blog/2019/08/ hazelnuts-where-and-when-to-forage/

Coulter, C. B. (2021, October 13). *Fall Fungi Foraging.* Pennsylvania Parks and Forests Foundation. Retrieved June 28, 2022, from https://paparksandforests.org/news/fallfungi-foraging/

Dandelion Foraging: Identification, look-a-likes, and Uses. (2020, June 10). Grow Forage Cook Ferment. Retrieved June 6, 2022, from https://www.growforagecookferment.com/ foraging-for-dandelions/

Dandelion | Garden Organic. (n.d.). Garden Organic |. Retrieved June 6, 2022, from https://www.garde norganic.org.uk/weeds/dandelion

Davis, E. M. (n.d.). *| Wild Food Girl. |* Wild Food Girl. Retrieved June 28, 2022, from https://wildfood girl.com/tag/pennsylvania/

Deane, G. (n.d.). *Chickasaw Plum: Yum - Eat The Weeds and other things, too.* Eat the Weeds. Retrieved June 28, 2022, from https://www.eattheweeds.com/chickasaw-plum-yum/

Delaware Facts & Symbols - Delaware Geography. (n.d.). Delaware.gov. Retrieved June 8, 2022, from https://de.gov/topics/facts/geo.shtml#:~

Demers, A. (n.d.). *Foraging Tours and Classes in Delaware.* Eat The Planet. Retrieved June 8, 2022, from https://eattheplanet.org/foraging-tours-and-classes-in-delaware/

Demers, A. (n.d.). *Foraging Tours and Classes in New Jersey.* Eat The Planet. Retrieved June 15, 2022, from https://eattheplanet.org/foraging-tours-and-classes-in-new-jersey/ Demers, A. (n.d.). *Foraging Tours and Classes in Pennsylvania.* Eat The Planet. RetrievedJune 27, 2022, from https://eattheplanet.org/ foraging-tours-and-classes-inpennsylvania/

Demers, A. (n.d.). *Foraging Tours and Classes in Virginia.* Eat The Planet. Retrieved June 28, 2022, from https://eattheplanet.org/foraging-tours-and-classes-in-virginia/

Demers, A. (n.d.). *Japanese Barberry, Invasive Winter Fruit.* Eat The Planet. Retrieved June 27, 2022, from https://eattheplanet.org/japanese-barberry-invasive-winter-fruit/

Dilawar, A. (n.d.). *Guided Foraging in the Hudson Valley.* Scenic Hudson. Retrieved June 22, 2022, from https://www.scenichudson.org/viewfinder/guided-foraging-inthe-hudson-valley/

Discover the climate and geography of New Jersey. (n.d.). World Travel Guide. Retrieved June 15, 2022, from https://www.worldtravelguide.net/guides/north-america/unitedstates-of-america/new-jersey/ weather-climate-geography/

Douglas, J. (2021, May 6). *Ethical Foraging- Responsibility and Reciprocity.* Organic Growers School. Retrieved June 3, 2022, from https://organicgrowersschool.org/ethical-foraging-responsibility-and-reciprocity/Eblen, S. (n.d.). Courier Post Online. Retrieved June 15, 2022, from https://eu. courier-postonline.com/story/life/2016/09/21/foraging-food-edibles-deptford/ 90494736/

The Edible Garden — Drying and Storing Your Herbs. (2010, October 5). YouTube. Retrieved July 1, 2022, from https://www.youtube.com/watch?v=mcNFGqZzm8o

Edible Wild Food Blog » Natural Mosquito Repellant – Bloodroot. (2012, May 7). Edible Wild Food. Retrieved June 30, 2022, from https://www.ediblewildfood.com/blog/2012/ 05/natural-mosquito-repellant-bloodroot/

Ellis, E. (2020, May 7). *Eating Wild in Virginia.* Oak Spring Garden Foundation. Retrieved June 29, 2022, from https://www.osgf.org/blog/2020/5/4/eating-wild-foraging-invirginia

Engels, J. (n.d.). *Forage for Dinner: Chicken of the Woods, a Magnificent Mushroom.* One Green Planet. Retrieved June 9, 2022, from https://www.onegreenplanet.org/ lifestyle/forage-for-dinner-chicken-of-the-woods/

Environment of West Virginia. (n.d.). Wikipedia. Retrieved June 29, 2022, from https://en. wikipedi-a.org/wiki/Environment_of_West_Virginia

Everett, W. (2021, July 8). *Foraging for Wild Strawberries • Insteading.* Insteading. Retrieved June 9, 2022, from https://insteading.com/blog/foraging-for-wild-strawberries/ Everett, W. (2021, July 26). *Foraging for Pokeweed • Insteading.* Insteading. Retrieved June23, 2022, from https://insteading.com/ blog/foraging-for-pokeweed/

Farrell, K. (2021, September 20). *Beach Plum Jam.* Fare Isle. Retrieved June 20, 2022, from https://fareisle. com/beach-plum-jam/

Farrell, K. (2022, May 6). *Candied Violets Recipe.* Fare Isle. Retrieved June 10, 2022, from https://fareisle. com/candied-violets/

5 Common Look-Alike Plants to Avoid When Wild Foraging. (2019, October 29). YouTube. Retrieved June 3, 2022, from https://www.youtube.com/watch?v=FsbrPKWj38Y

Foraged Food Recipes - Cook. (n.d.). Grow Forage Cook Ferment. Retrieved July 1, 2022, from https:// www.growforagecookferment.com/cook/foraged-food-recipes/ *Foraging Aronia Berries, Wild Super Food |.* (2014, September 5). One Acre Farm. Retrieved June 9, 2022, from https://ouroneacrefarm. com/2014/09/05/foraging-aronia-berries/

Foraging & Feasting. (n.d.). Facebook. Retrieved June 30, 2022, from https://z-upload. facebook.-com/ForagingFeasting/posts/4302190783224701

Foraging for Acorns: Identification, Processing + Acorn Recipes. (2018, October 20). Grow Forage Cook Ferment. Retrieved June 13, 2022, from https://www. growforagecookferment.com/foraging-for-acorns/

Foraging for Chicory. (2016, October 6). Grow Forage Cook Ferment. Retrieved June 29, 2022, from https://www.growforagecookferment.com/foraging-for-chicory/

Foraging for Mugwort. (2016, June 5). Grow Forage Cook Ferment. Retrieved June 23, 2022, from https://www.growforagecookferment.com/foraging-for-mugwort/

Foraging for Pineapple Weed (Wild Chamomile) + Pineapple Weed Tea. (2018, June 15). Grow Forage Cook Ferment. Retrieved June 29, 2022, from https://www. growforagecookferment.com/foraging-pineapple-weed/

Foraging for Purple Dead Nettle: an edible backyard weed. (2020, April 10). Grow Forage Cook Ferment. Retrieved June 15, 2022, from https://www.growforagecookferment. com/foraging-purple-dead-nettle/

Foraging for Wild, Natural, Organic Food: Chestnuts. (2009, October 6). The 3 Foragers. Retrieved June 15, 2022, from http://the3foragers.blogspot.com/2009/10/ chestnuts.html

Foraging for Wild Violets: an edible early spring flower. (2021, February 26). Grow Forage Cook Ferment. Retrieved June 9, 2022, from https://www.growforagecookferment. com/foraging-for-wild-violets/

Foraging Guidelines. (n.d.). Woodland Trust. Retrieved June 3, 2022, from https://www. woodlandtrust.org.uk/visiting-woods/things-to-do/foraging/foraging-guidelines/ *Foraging Guide Wood Blewit | UK Foraging.* (n.d.). The Foraging Course Company. Retrieved June 15, 2022, from https:// www.foragingcoursecompany.co.uk/foragingguide-wood-blewit

Foraging in Jersey | Inspiration. (n.d.). Visit Jersey. Retrieved June 15, 2022, from https:// www.jersey.com/inspire-me/inspiration/foraging-in-jersey/

Foraging in Southern West Virginia - Visit Southern West Virginia. (2022, April 6). Visit Southern West Virginia. Retrieved June 29, 2022, from https://visitwv.com/ foraging/

Foraging in Southern West Virginia - Visit Southern West Virginia. (2022, April 6). Visit Southern West Virginia. Retrieved June 30, 2022, from https://visitwv.com/ foraging/

Foraging Plantain: Identification and Uses. (2020, July 28). Grow Forage Cook Ferment. Retrieved June 23, 2022, from https://www.growforagecookferment.com/plantainnatures-band-aid/

Foraging Wild Fruit: Black Cherry. (2013, August 13). JOSH FECTEAU. Retrieved June 9, 2022, from https://joshfecteau.com/foraging-wild-fruit-black-cherry/

Foraging Wild Fruit: Highbush Blueberry. (2013, July 31). JOSH FECTEAU. Retrieved June 15, 2022, from https://joshfecteau.com/foraging-wild-fruit-highbush-blueberry/ Gaddy, K. (2018, May 1). *A Guide to Wild Edibles in West Virginia.* Culture Trip. Retrieved. June 30, 2022, from https://theculturetrip. com/north-america/usa/westvirginia/ articles/a-guide-to-wild-edibles-in-west-virginia/

Gambrell, H. (2019, March 4). *Food foraging tours in Virginia.* Northern Virginia Magazine. Retrieved June 28, 2022, from https://northernvirginiamag.com/things-to-do/ travel/2019/03/04/4-foraging-tours-every-virginia-foodie-should-consider/ Garce, K. (n.d.). *How to Forage Black Walnuts: The Complete Guide.* FoodsForAntiAging.com. Retrieved June 13, 2022, from https://foodsforantiaging. com/how-to-forage-black-walnuts-the-complete-guide/

Gardiner, B. (2021, February 14). *9 Basic Principles Of Ethical Wildcrafting For Beginners.* The Outdoor Apothecary. Retrieved June 3, 2022, from https://www. outdoorapothecary.com/ethical-wildcrafting/

Gardner, J. A. (2015, May 14). *Foraging for Wild Dandelion Greens – Mother Earth News.* Mother Earth News. Retrieved June 6, 2022, from https://www.motherearthnews. com/organic-gardening/foraging-for-wild-dandelion-greens-zbcz1505/

Geography of New York (state). (n.d.). Wikipedia. Retrieved June 22, 2022, from https://en. wikipedia.org/wiki/Geography_of_New_York_(state)

Geography of Pennsylvania. (n.d.). Wikipedia. Retrieved June 27, 2022, from https://en. wikipedia.org/wiki/Geography_of_Pennsylvania

Ginseng Chicken Soup: The Ultimate Nourishing Soup for Energy, Brain Function and Immune Support. (2019, February 22). Yang's Nourishing Kitchen. Retrieved June 30, 2022, from https://www.yangsnourishingkitchen.com/ginseng-chicken-soup/

Grafton, W. N. (n.d.). *Elderberries - West Virginia Division of Natural Resources.* West Virginia Division of Natural Resources. Retrieved June 30, 2022, from https://wvdnr. gov/outdoor-recreation/plants-fungi/elderberries/

Grant, A. (2021, October 18). *Can You Forage For Ginseng: Learn How To Pick Wild Ginseng Root.* Gardening Know How. Retrieved June 30, 2022, from https://www. gardeningknowhow.com/edible/herbs/ginseng/is-foraging-for-ginseng-legal.htm

Growing and Foraging for Raspberries (and their leaves!). (2015, July 21). Grow Forage Cook Ferment. Retrieved June 23, 2022, from https://www.growforagecookferment.com/ growing-and-foraging-for-raspberries/

Halbkat, C. (2022, March 12). *Ramps: How to Forage & Eat Wild Leeks.* Wild Edible. Retrieved June 13, 2022, from https://www.wildedible.com/blog/foraging-ramps Hard, L. (2015, July 11). *All About Foraged Fruit - How to Find and Use Mulberries.* Food52. Retrieved June 9, 2022, from https://food52. com/blog/13462-mulberriesthe-fruit-that-s-probably-growing-in-your-yard-right-now

Harkins, T. (2021, August 31). *How to Forage and Use Sassafras • New Life On A Homestead*. New Life On A Homestead. Retrieved June 9, 2022, from https://www. newlifeonahomestead.com/sassafras/

Hickory Nut Foraging - How To Harvest And Use Carya Fruits. (n.d.). DIYS.com. Retrieved June 29, 2022, from https://www.diys.com/hickory-nut/

How to Find, Identify and Cook Fiddleheads. (n.d.). Fearless Eating. Retrieved June 27, 2022, from https://fearlesseating.net/fiddleheads/

How to Harvest, Process, and Store Foraged Greens. (n.d.). Forager Chef. Retrieved July 1, 2022, from https://foragerchef.com/how-i-forage-and-store-wild-greens-plants-andherbs/

Identify Field Garlic - Foraging for Wild Edible Plants — Good Life Revival. (2017, March 21). Good Life Revival. Retrieved June 23, 2022, from https://thegoodliferevival. com/blog/wild-field-garlic

Identify Garlic Mustard - Foraging for Wild Edible Greens — Good Life Revival. (2017, May 23). Good Life Revival. Retrieved June 14, 2022, from https://thegoodliferevival. com/blog/garlic-mustard

How to Make Shaggy Mane Mushroom Ink. (n.d.). Forager Chef. Retrieved June 28, 2022, from https://foragerchef.com/shaggy-mane-ink/

How to Pick and Prepare Purslane. (2002, June 19). The Washington Post. Retrieved June 6, 2022, from https://www.washingtonpost.com/archive/lifestyle/food/2002/06/19/ how-to-pick-and-prepare-purslane/5109fc88-1282-4072-8539-a2321798ac2b/

How to Safely Forage. (2018, November 28). Institute of Culinary Education. Retrieved June 3, 2022, from https://ice.edu/blog/how-to-safely-forage

Huffstetler, E. (n.d.). *Storing Nuts Properly - Food Storage*. The Spruce Eats. Retrieved July 1, 2022, from https://www.thespruceeats.com/how-to-store-nuts-1389147

Huffstetler, E. (2020, October 5). *How to Harvest Pecans Yourself*. The Spruce Eats. Retrieved June 30, 2022, from https://www.thespruceeats.com/how-to-harvestpecans-yourself-1388178

Hunting and cooking honey mushrooms, honey fungus, or Armillaria mellea. (n.d.). Forager Chef. Retrieved June 15, 2022, from https://foragerchef.com/honey-mushrooms-thepride-of-eastern-europe/

Invasive Hardy Kiwi: An Emerging Invasive in the Northeastern United States. (n.d.). Northeastern IPM Center. Retrieved June 27, 2022, from https://www.northeastipm. org/ipm-in-action/publications/invasive-hardy-kiwi/

Kent, S. (2018, August 22). *N.J.'s wild mushrooms are poisoning people at a staggering rate. Here's what to avoid*. NJ.com. Retrieved June 20, 2022, from https://www.nj.com/ news/2018/08/why_is_there_a_spike_in_mushrooms_poisonings_in_ne.html

Kettlewell, C. (2014, August 18). *Fungi Roulette - VirginiaLiving.com*. Virginia Living. Retrieved June 29, 2022, from https://www.virginialiving.com/fungi-roulette/

Kiffel, J. (n.d.). *New Jersey Pictures and Facts*. National Geographic Kids. Retrieved June 15, 2022, from https://kids.nationalgeographic.com/geography/states/article/newjersey

Kornegay, M. (2015, October 7). *What's a Kiwi Berry? Weaver's Orchard Knows! — PA Eats*. PA Eats. Retrieved June 27, 2022, from https://www.paeats.org/news/2015/whatsa-kiwi-berry-weaversorchard-knows/

Kovach, E. (n.d.). *The PA Eats Guide to Foraging in Pennsylvania | Foraging Wild Foods*. PA Eats. Retrieved June 27, 2022, from https://www.paeats.org/feature/foraging-inpennsylvania/

Kusby, A. (2017, May 24). *Foraging For Morels? Here's What You Need To Know*. Garden Collage. Retrieved June 14, 2022, from https://gardencollage.com/nourish/farm-totable/everything-need-know-morel-mushroom-foraging/

Larsen, L. (2018, October 22). *Chestnut Stuffing Recipe*. The Spruce Eats. Retrieved June 20, 2022, from https://www.thespruceeats.com/chestnut-stuffing-482788

Lindell, J. (2017, September 21). *Common Indiana Maple Trees*. Garden Guides. Retrieved June 29, 2022, from https://www.gardenguides.com/95691-common-indiana-mapletrees.html

Lubiner, V., & Brellis, D. (2020, July 5). *The Foraged Berries Series: Identify and Harvest Wineberries – Natural History Society of Maryland*. Natural History Society of Maryland. Retrieved June 13, 2022, from https://www.marylandnature.org/the-foragedberries-series-how-to-identify-and-harvest-wineberries/

Luther, L. (n.d.). *Oyster Mushrooms - Edible Wild Mushroom - Western PA Foraging*. Luther Homestead. Retrieved June 28, 2022, from https://www.luthertravels.com/oystermushrooms-in-pa/

Lynn, J. (2020, August 20). *Edible mushrooms start to sprout in Delaware Valley*. WHYY. Retrieved June 9, 2022, from https://whyy.org/articles/edible-mushrooms-startsprouting-across-delaware-valley-after-rainy-summer-months/

Mallow - A Foraging Guide to Its Food, Medicine and Other Uses. (n.d.). Eatweeds. Retrieved June 15, 2022, from https://www.eatweeds.co.uk/mallow-malva-sylvestris

Marion, J., & Tsucalas, J. (2015, June 3). *Local Foragers Go Into the Woods*. Baltimore Magazine. Retrieved June 10, 2022, from https://www.baltimoremagazine.com/ section/fooddrink/local-foragers-go-into-the-woods/

Maryland - Global Climate. (2022, June 2). Climate Policy Watcher. Retrieved June 10, 2022, from https:// www.climate-policy-watcher.org/global-climate-2/maryland-1.html

Maryland Topography | *VisitMaryland.org*. (n.d.). Visit Maryland. Retrieved June 10, 2022, from https://www.visitmaryland.org/info/maryland-topography

Medicinal Shrubs: Japanese Barberry. (2014, November 3). JOSH FECTEAU. Retrieved June 30, 2022, from https://joshfecteau.com/medicinal-shrubs-japanese-barberry/

Meredith, L. (n.d.). *Chicken of the Woods Pasta Sauce Recipe – Mother Earth News*. Mother Earth News. Retrieved June 10, 2022, from https://www.motherearthnews.com/realfood/seasonal-recipes/chicken-of-the-woods-pasta-sauce-zerz1610zfis

Meredith, L. (2014, December 4). *Cold-Weather Foraging for Wild, American Persimmons – Mother Earth News*. Mother Earth News. Retrieved June 9, 2022, from https://www.motherearthnews.com/real-food/foraging-for-wild-american-persimmonszbcz1412/

Meredith, L. (2019, June 3). *11 Great Ways to Preserve Berries*. The Spruce Eats. Retrieved July 1, 2022, from https://www.thespruceeats.com/how-to-preserve-berries-1327687 Meredith, L. (2020, June 19). *Foraging for Juneberries, and Juneberry Pie Recipe – Mother Earth News*. Mother Earth News. Retrieved June 9, 2022, from https://www.motherearthnews.com/real-food/foraging-for-juneberries-and-juneberry-pie-recipe-zbcz1506/ Mitchell, C. W. (n.d.). *Maryland*. Wikipedia. Retrieved June 10, 2022, from https://en.wikipedia.org/wiki/Maryland

Nannyberry Butter or Puree. (n.d.). Forager Chef. Retrieved June 29, 2022, from https://foragerchef.com/nannyberry-maple-butter/

New Jersey. (n.d.). Wikipedia. Retrieved June 15, 2022, from https://en.wikipedia.org/wiki/New_Jersey#Geography

New York climate: weather by month, temperature, precipitation, when to go. (n.d.). Climates to Travel. Retrieved June 22, 2022, from https://www.climatestotravel.com/climate/united-states/new-york

Noyes, L. (2020, September 24). *Foraging For Autumn Olive Berries & 11 Recipes To Make*. Rural Sprout. Retrieved June 13, 2022, from https://www.ruralsprout.com/autumnolive-berries/

Olson, K. (2020, August 6). *Yellow Sweet Clover: Information and Management*. SDSU Extension. Retrieved June 15, 2022, from https://extension.sdstate.edu/yellow-sweetclover-information-and-management

Orr, E. (n.d.). *Jerusalem Artichoke or Sunchoke (Helianthus tuberosus)*. Wild Edible. Retrieved June 29, 2022, from https://www.wildedible.com/wild-food-guide/jerusalem-artichoke Orr, E. (n.d.). *Watercress: How to find, identify and forage*. Wild Edible. Retrieved June 6, 2022, from https://www.wildedible.com/wild-food-guide/watercress

Orr, E. (n.d.). *Wood Sorrel* | *Foraging for Wild Edibles*. Wild Edible. Retrieved June 13, 2022, from https://www.wildedible.com/wild-food-guide/wood-sorrel

Ovenden, S. (n.d.). *Foraging: A beginner's guide*. BBC Good Food. Retrieved July 1, 2022, from https://www.bbcgoodfood.com/howto/guide/foraging

Painter, S. (n.d.). *Growing and Harvest Purslane* | *LoveToKnow*. Garden. Retrieved June 6, 2022, from https://garden.lovetoknow.com/wiki/Purslane

Passiflora caerulea (Blue Passion Flower). (n.d.). Gardenia.net. Retrieved June 28, 2022, from https://www.gardenia.net/plant/passiflora-caerulea-blue-passion-flower

Passionflower's Medicinal & Edible Uses | *Chestnut School*. (2022, May 26). Chestnut School of Herbal Medicine. Retrieved June 28, 2022, from https://chestnutherbs.com/passionflower-ecology-cultivation-botany-and-medicinal-and-edible-uses/

Pennsylvania - Climate | *Britannica*. (n.d.). Encyclopedia Britannica. Retrieved June 27, 2022, from https://www.britannica.com/place/Pennsylvania-state/Climate

Pennsylvania Maps & Facts. (2021, February 25). World Atlas. Retrieved June 27, 2022, from https://www.worldatlas.com/maps/united-states/pennsylvania

Perfect For Mushroom Foraging Beginners! — *Book Wild Food Foraging Classes Online*. (2019, October 25). Forage SF. Retrieved June 25, 2022, from https://www.foragesf.com/blog/2019/10/25/black-trumpet-mushrooms-perfect-for-mushroom-foragingbeginners

Petrocelly, S. (2021, September 8). *5 Tips for Foraging Wild Pawpaws*. Wichita, KS. Retrieved June 15, 2022, from https://ourcommunitynow.com/home-and-garden/5tips-for-foraging-wild-pawpaws

Pickled Hen of the Woods Mushroom Recipe. (n.d.). Forager Chef. Retrieved June 29, 2022, from https://foragerchef.com/pickled-hen-of-the-woods-mushroomsmaitake/

Pickled Rosehips - Recipes. (2019, August 26). Eatweeds. Retrieved June 28, 2022, from https://www.eatweeds.co.uk/pickled-rosehips

Pilarski, M. (n.d.). *Goldenseal – Hydrastis canadensis*. United Plant Savers. Retrieved June 30, 2022, from https://unitedplantsavers.org/species-at-risk-list/goldensealhydrastis-canadensis-2/

Preston, M. (n.d.). *Japanese Knotweed: The Massively Destructive Weed That Chefs Love* | *Bon Appétit*. Bon Appétit. Retrieved June 27, 2022, from https://www.bonappetit.com/test-kitchen/ingredients/article/japanese-knotweed-recipes#:~

Purslane Identification — *Four Season Foraging*. (2018, July 24). Four Season Foraging. Retrieved June 6, 2022, from https://www.fourseasonforaging.com/blog/2018/7/24/purslane-identification

Raver, A. (2008, July 3). *Foraging for Berries, the Summer Special on Nature's Produce Aisle (Published 2008)*.

The New York Times. Retrieved June 22, 2022, from https://www. nytimes.com/2008/07/03/garden/03garden.html

Rebholz, M., Hawk, A., Wiley, E., Panas, A., Wietor, K., Sweeny, B., Kolkedy, S., & Broverman, J. (2021, September 22). *Paw Paw Season in West Virginia*. Weelunk. Retrieved June 30, 2022, from https:// weelunk.com/paw-paw-season-west-virginia/ *Roasted Chicory Root "Coffee"*. (n.d.). Hunger and Thirst. Retrieved July 1, 2022, from http://hungerandthirstforlife.blogspot.com/2013/10/roasted-chicory-root-coffee.html Roesler, J. (n.d.). *Hen of the Woods or Maitake Mushrooms*. Forager Chef. Retrieved June 29, 2022, from https://foragerchef.com/hen-of-the-woods-mushrooms/

Roesler, J., & Beard, J. (n.d.). *Foraging and Cooking Shaggy Mane Mushrooms*. Forager Chef. Retrieved June 28, 2022, from https://foragerchef.com/the-shaggy-mane-mushroomlawyers-wig/

Rosehip - A Foraging Guide to Its Food, Medicine and Other Uses. (n.d.). Eatweeds. Retrieved June 27, 2022, from https://www.eatweeds.co.uk/rosehip-rosa-canina

Sand Hickory. (2012, September 19). Augusta, GA. Retrieved June 29, 2022, from https:// www.augusta-ga.gov/1628/Sand-Hickory

Schneck, M. (2018, October 22). *15 things you don't know about nuts in Pennsylvania*. PennLive.com. Retrieved June 27, 2022, from https://www.pennlive.com/ wildaboutpa/2018/10/15_things_you_-dont_know_about_3.html

7 Wild Mushrooms in PA | Wild Pennsylvania Mushrooms You Can Eat. (n.d.). Luther Homestead. Retrieved June 27, 2022, from https://www.lutherhomestead.com/7-amazingwild-mushrooms-in-pa/

Sexton, S. (2018, September 11). *Top 10 Most Dangerous Plant look-a-likes - The Grow Network*. The Grow Network. Retrieved June 3, 2022, from https://thegrownetwork. com/most-dangerous-plant-look-a-likes/

Shaw, H. (n.d.). *Edible Wild Plants and Mushrooms - Recipes and Guides | Hank Shaw*. Hunter Angler Gardener Cook. Retrieved June 26, 2022, from https://honest-food. net/foraging-recipes/

Shaw, H. (n.d.). *Elderberry Liqueur Recipe - How to Make Elderberry Liqueur | Hank Shaw*. Hunter Angler Gardener Cook. Retrieved June 30, 2022, from https://honest-food. net/foraging-recipes/sweets-and-syrups/elderberry-liqueur/

Shrimp of the Woods Mushrooms or Aborted Entolomas. (n.d.). Forager Chef. Retrieved June 28, 2022, from https://foragerchef.com/entoloma-abortivum-aborted-entolomamushroom/

Spicebush Berries, aka Lindera Benzoin. (2017, July 9). Backyard Forager. Retrieved June 27, 2022, from https://backyardforager.com/spicebush-berries-lindera-benzoin/

Spring Ephemeral Wildflowers of the Southeast. (2021, January 23). Feral Foraging. Retrieved June 30, 2022, from https://feralforaging.com/spring-ephemeral-wildflowers-of-thesoutheast/

Stafford, A. (2007, October 11). *Super Moist Pawpaw Quick Bread*. Alexandra's Kitchen. Retrieved June 30, 2022, from https://alexandracooks.com/2007/10/11/pawpaws/ *Strawberry and Japanese Knotweed Crisp*. (2017, May 5). Very Vegan Val. Retrieved June 28, 2022, from https://veryveganval.com/2017/05/05/strawberry-and-japaneseknotweed-crisp/

Sumac Foraging and Preparation. (2018, August 15). The Chopping Block. Retrieved June 9, 2022, from https://www.thechoppingblock.com/blog/sumac-foraging-and-preparation-0

Swecker, C. (2017, May 9). *Picking Wild Edibles like Ramps and Other Legal Activities in the Monongahela National Forest*. Allegheny Mountain Radio. Retrieved June 29, 2022, from https://www.allegheny mountainradio.org/picking-wild-edibles-like-rampsand-other-legal-activities-in-the-monongahela-national-forest/

Tenaglia, D., & Moore, D. (n.d.). *Watercress (Nasturtium officinale)*. USDA Forest Service. Retrieved June 6, 2022, from https://www.fs.fed.us/wildflowers/plant-of-the-week/ nasturtium_officinale.shtml

Tkaczyk, F. (n.d.). *Lobster Mushroom Basics*. Alderleaf Wilderness College. Retrieved June 26, 2022, from https://www.wildernesscollege.com/lobster-mushroom.html

Townsend, J., & Anderson, C. (2019, July 28). *Edible and Medicinal Wild Plants of Western New York – Chautauqua Watershed Conservancy*. Chautauqua Watershed Conservancy. Retrieved June 22, 2022, from https://chau tauquawatershed.org/2019/07/28/ edible-and-medicinal-wild-plants-of-western-new-york/

Trees of the Adirondacks: Black Cherry | Prunus serotina. (n.d.). Adirondack Nature. Retrieved June 23, 2022, from https://wildadirondacks.org/trees-of-the-adirondacksblack-cherry-prunus-serotina.html

20-Minute Berry Jam - foodiecrush .com. (n.d.). Foodie Crush. Retrieved July 1, 2022, from https://www. foodiecrush.com/20-minute-berry-jam/

The Ultimate Guide: How to Forage and Cook Chanterelle Mushrooms. (2020, July 16). Mossy Oak. Retrieved June 14, 2022, from https://www.mossyoak.com/our-obsession/ blogs/how-to/the-ultimate-guide-how-to-forage-and-cook-chanterelle-mushrooms

Universal Edibility Test: How to Test a Wild Plant's Edibility - 2022. (2022, March 2). MasterClass. Retrieved June 3, 2022, from https://www.masterclass.com/articles/ universal-edibility-test#what-is-the-universal-edibility-test

Upper Delaware River, a Foraging Gig – Part 1 I *Coriolistic Anachronisms Mobile*. (2014, May 28). Vincent Mounier Photography. Retrieved June 8, 2022, from https://www. vincentmounier.com/blog2/upper-delaware-river-foraging/

Vanheems, B. (2021, September 24). *The Best Ways to Store Root Vegetables*. GrowVeg.com. Retrieved July 1, 2022, from https://www.growveg.co.za/guides/the-best-ways-tostore-root-vegetables/

Virginia. (n.d.). Wikipedia. Retrieved June 28, 2022, from https://en.wikipedia.org/wiki/ Virginia

Virginia - Climate I *Britannica*. (n.d.). Encyclopedia Britannica. Retrieved June 28, 2022, from https:// www.britannica.com/place/Virginia-state/Climate

von Frank, A. (2018, February 17). *Chickweed recipe: turning common weeds into gourmet food*. Tyrant Farms. Retrieved June 20, 2022, from https://www.tyrantfarms.com/ chickweed-recipe-turning-common-weeds-into-gourmet-food/

Vos, H. (n.d.). *The Regions of Virginia* I *Virginia Museum of History & Culture*. Virginia Historical Society. Retrieved June 28, 2022, from https://virginiahistory.org/learn/ regions-virginia

Walker, D., & Tidwell, M. (2017, August 11). *How to Keep Berries Fresh for Longer (Tutorial, Save Time and Money)*. Against All Grain. Retrieved July 1, 2022, from https:// againstallgrain.com/2017/08/11/how-to-keep-berries-fresh-longer/

Weese, M., & Demers, A. (n.d.). *Foraging Tours and Classes in Maryland*. Eat The Planet. Retrieved June 10, 2022, from https://eattheplanet.org/foraging-tours-and-classesin-maryland/

West Virginia. (n.d.). Wikipedia. Retrieved June 29, 2022, from https://en.wikipedia.org/ wiki/West_Virginia#Separation_from_Virginia

What is the weather, climate and geography like in West Virginia. (n.d.). World Travel Guide. Retrieved June 29, 2022, from https://www.worldtravelguide.net/guides/northamerica/united-states-of-america/west-virginia/weather-climate-geography/ *What's in season: watercress*. (n.d.). Diabetes UK. Retrieved June 6, 2022, from https:// www.diabetes.org.uk/guide-to-diabetes/enjoy-food/cooking-for-people-withdiabetes/seasonal-cooking/whats-in-season-watercress

Wild Blueberries: A Gateway Food. (2017, July 23). Backyard Forager. Retrieved June 9, 2022, from https:// backyardforager.com/wild-blueberries-a-gateway-food/

Wild Food: How to Forage and Store Wild Greens. (n.d.). Chelsea Green Publishing. Retrieved June 30, 2022, from https://www.chelseagreen.com/2021/how-to-forageand-store-wild-greens/

Wild Foraging. (n.d.). Maryland DNR. Retrieved June 14, 2022, from https://dnr. maryland.gov/cookbook/Pages/wild-foraging.aspx

Wild Plants With Toxic Look Alikes - Toxic Plant Guide. (2019, June 24). RV Life. Retrieved June 3, 2022, from https://rvlife.com/wild-plants/

Wild recipes from public lands across the country. (2018, April 2). US Department of the Interior. Retrieved June 30, 2022, from https://www.doi.gov/blog/wild-recipes-publiclands-across-country

Williams, C. (2019, December 30). *What Is Watercress and What Does It Taste Like?* MyRecipes. Retrieved June 6, 2022, from https://www.myrecipes.com/how-to/ cooking-questions/what-is-watercress

Williams, M. (2021, October 21). *Storing Up for Winter with Forageables* I *Virginia DWR*. Virginia Department of Wildlife Resources. Retrieved June 29, 2022, from https:// dwr.virginia.gov/blog/storing-up-for-winter-with-forageables/

Wilson, D. R. (n.d.). *Dandelion: Health Benefits and Side Effects*. Healthline. Retrieved June 6, 2022, from https://www.healthline.com/nutrition/dandelion-benefits

Winter Foraging: Barberry – The Resistance Garden. (2019, December 4). The Resistance Garden. Retrieved June 27, 2022, from https://www.theresistancegarden.com/ barberry/

Wong, T. M. (n.d.). *Foraged Flavor: Wild Hickory Nuts*. Serious Eats. Retrieved June 13, 2022, from https:// www.seriouseats.com/foraged-flavor-wild-hickory-nuts

Oakland County, MI Government. (2021, November 4). *Pokeweed: Facts, Folklore and Warnings*. Oakland County Blog. https://oaklandcountyblog.com/2016/09/16/ pokeweed-facts-folklore-and-warnings/

Bloodroot I *Encyclopedia.com*. (n.d.). Encyclopedia.Com. https://www.encyclopedia.com/plants-and-animals/plants/plants/bloodroot#:%7E:text=Bloodroot%20has%20a% 20long%20history,%2C%20growths%2C%20and%20cancerous%20tumors.

Lubiner, V. (2020, November 8). *Burdock—a weed, a medicine, and a delicacy. – Natural History Society of Maryland*. Natural History Society of Maryland. https://www. marylandnature.org/burdock-a-weed-a-medicine-and-a-delicacy/

Singh, M. (2021, July 10). *Chickweed benefits for dogs*. Yourolddog. https://yourolddog. com/chickweed-benefits-for-dogs/

Gaeng, J. (2022, February 11). *Are Dandelions Poisonous To Dogs Or Cats?* AZ Animals. https://a-z-animals.com/blog/are-dandelions-poisonous-to-dogs-or-cats/

Dooryard Violet (Viola communis). (n.d.). iNaturalist. https://www.inaturalist.org/taxa/ 1391871-Viola-communis#cite_note-nozeda297-7

Cornell University Department of Animal Science. (n.d.). Cornell CALS. https:// poisonousplants.ansci.cornell.edu/toxicagents/glucosin.html

Care, T. P. (2019, October 3). Ginseng. Treatwell Pet Care Learning Centre. https://learn. treatwellpetcare.ca/article/817-ginseng#:%7E:text=Ginseng%20is%20commonly%   20prescribed%20to,minimize%20stress%20in%20any%20animal.

Nordqvist, J. (2021, May 17). What are the health benefits of ginseng? Medical News Today. https://www. medicalnewstoday.com/articles/262982#side-effects

Goldenseal, Hydrastis Canadensis L.: A Long And Colorful Folk History Native Plant. (n.d.). Mecklenburg Extension Master Gardener^SM Volunteers. https://www.mastergarden ersmecklenburg.org/goldenseal-hydrastis-canadensis-l-a-long-and-colorful-folkhistory-native-plant.html#:%7E:text=Cherokee%20Indians%20used%20Goldenseal%   20root,pneumonia%20and%20several%20digestive%20disorders.

Wikipedia contributors. (2022, July 2). Mugwort. Wikipedia. https://en.wikipedia.org/ wiki/Mugwort

Can Dogs Eat Fiddleheads? | Benefits, Risks. (n.d.). Can Dogs Eat It. https://www. candogseatit.com/fruitveg/fiddleheads

Keenan, J. (2021, December 15). The Secrets Of Plantain For Dogs. Dogs Naturally. https:// www.dogsnaturallymagazine.com/can-dogs-eat-plantain/

McNally, D. (2022, May 24). Can Dogs Eat Purslane? Is Purslane Safe For Dogs? DogTime. https://dogtime. com/dog-health/dog-food-dog-nutrition/96248-can-dogs-eatpurslane-safe#:%7E:text=The%   20short%20answer%20is%20no,It%20is%20actually%20very%20toxic.&text=If%20you%20suspect%20your%20dog,them%20to%20the%20vet%20immediately.

Health Benefits of Purslane. (2020, September 23). WebMD. https://www.webmd.com/ diet/health-benefits-purslane#:%7E:text=It%20is%20one%20of%20the,of%20any%20land%2Dbased%20plant.

Hamburger icon. (n.d.). Wag Walking. https://wagwalking.com/condition/leeks-poisoning#:%7E:text=   The%20leek%20(Allium%20ampeloprasum)%20is,blood%20cells%2C%20producing%20hemolytic%20anemia.

Can Dogs Eat Sassafras? | Health Risks. (n.d.). Can Dogs Eat It. https://www. candogseatit.com/herbs-spices/sassafras#:%7E:text=Sassafras%20contains%   20safrole%2C%20a%20toxic,damage%20and%20cancer%20in%20dogs.

D. (2022, April 16). Sacred Tree Profile: The Medicine, Magic, and Uses of Staghorn Sumac (Rhus Typhina). The Druids Garden. https://thedruidsgarden.com/2020/07/19/ sacred-tree-profile-staghorn-sumac-Rhus-typhina/

Rosa canina, Dog Rose: identification, distribution, habitat. (n.d.-b). https://www.first-nature.com/flowers/ rosa-canina.php

https://plants.usda.gov/DocumentLibrary/plantguide/pdf/pg_prma2.pdf

Home | North Carolina Extension Gardener Plant Toolbox. (n.d.). https://plants.ces.ncsu.edu/

Just a moment. . . (n.d.-b). https://www.wildflower.org/plants/

Can Dogs Eat Kiwiberry? | Benefits, Risks. (n.d.). Can Dogs Eat It. https://www.candogseatit.com/fruitveg/kiwiberry

Adamant, A. (2021, June 11). Foraging Black Chokeberry: Identification & Uses (Aronia melanocarpa). Practical Self Reliance. https://practicalselfreliance.com/black-chokeberry/

Butterfield, M. (2019, January 26). 10 Fun Facts About Raspberries! One Hundred Dollars a Month. https://www.onehundreddollarsamonth.com/10-fun-facts-about-raspberries/

Sepal. (2022, May 23). In Wikipedia. https://en.wikipedia.org/wiki/Sepal

Kitchen, M. (2021, February 2). Wine Berry - Rubus phoenicolasius. Mayernik Kitchen. https://www. mayernikkitchen.com/medicinal-plants/wine-berry

Harford, R. (2023, January 9). Common Mallow. EATWEEDS. https://www.eatweeds.co.uk/mallow-malva-sylvestris

NCBI - WWW Error Blocked Diagnostic. (n.d.). https://www.ncbi.nlm.nih.gov/pmc/articles/ PMC5878035/

Seitz, S. (2022, April 18). Purple Dead Nettle Uses, Benefits, and Recipes. Healthy Green Kitchen. https:// www.healthygreenkitchen.com/purple-dead-nettle-uses/

Academy, H. (2020, June 29). Purple Dead Nettle: Nutrition and Recipes –. Herbal Academy. https:// theherbalacademy.com/purple-dead-nettle/

Cornelia, C. (2022, April 8). Dead Nettle, an Overlooked yet Valuable Wild Edible. Eat the Planet. Retrieved January 23, 2023, from https://eattheplanet.org/dead-nettle-an-overlooked-yet-valuable-wild-edible/

O'Driscoll, D. (2022, April 16). Sacred Tree Profile: The Medicine, Magic, and Uses of Staghorn Sumac (Rhus Typhina). The Druids Garden. https://thedruidsgarden.com/2020/07/19/sacred-tree-profile-staghorn-sumac-rhus-typhina/

NCBI - WWW Error Blocked Diagnostic. (n.d.-b). https://www.ncbi.nlm.nih.gov/pmc/articles/ PMC8123986/

237

NCBI - WWW Error Blocked Diagnostic. (n.d.-c). https://www.ncbi.nlm.nih.gov/pmc/articles/PMC6270007/

Indigo Herbs. (2020, August 7). *Black Walnut Benefits.* https://www.indigo-herbs.co.uk/natural-health-guide/benefits/black-walnut

Health Benefits of Bolete Mushroom. (2022, November 18). WebMD. https://www.webmd.com/diet/benefits-of-bolete-mushroom

Harp, V. (2021, September 14). *King Bolete aka Penny Bun, Cep, or Porcini | Excellent Edible.* Oregon Discovery. Retrieved January 30, 2023, from https://oregondiscovery.com/king-bolete

Grifola frondosa. (2019, July 3). Midwest American Mycological Information. https://midwestmycology.org/grifola-frondosa/

NCBI - WWW Error Blocked Diagnostic. (n.d.-d). https://www.ncbi.nlm.nih.gov/pmc/articles/PMC7754439/

Made in the USA
Monee, IL
23 September 2024

66397413R00138